Acknowledgments

I would like to thank the many designers who allowed me to include their work in this edition, including those highlighted in Chapter 5: Antonio Alcalá, Michelle Bowers (no relation), Julie Beeler and Brad Johnson, Sol Sender, and Rick Valicenti. My sincere thanks to Margaret Cummins, senior editor at John Wiley & Sons; Lauren Poplawski, senior editorial assistant; and Doug Salvemini, production editor, for the production assistance; and Karin C. Warren for her help in developing the manuscript. Special thanks to my family, students, colleagues, and friends who gave their support to this project, especially Helene, Jackson, and Sofia.

John Bowers Introduction to Graphic Design Methodologies and Processes

Contents

Contents Overview

Front and Back

1
Looking Broadly

2
Interpreting

Contents Overview

John Bowers Introduction to Graphic Design Methodologies and Processes

Most graphic designers I know are cautious of graphic design methodologies and processes. They believe formalized approaches are akin to formulas or gimmicks that require little thought, hard work, or regard for the problem at hand. Little has been written on the subject for graphic design students. Yet we all have our own processes and benefit from advancements that are the result of research and methodologies.

Understanding, developing, and applying methodologies and processes can expand possibilities, develop your ideas, and better utilize your abilities. This can lead to work that is original, appropriate, inspiring, and responsible.

My formal education was largely based on developing my intuition through a simple problem-solving approach. While that has served me well, early on I benefited from exposure to design approaches from the Design Management Conference proceedings. Later professional experience at Landor also expanded my interest and understanding. There, I worked alongside consultants who researched specific audiences to achieve desired responses. Since then, I've learned on my own by reading, attending lectures, talking with others, and paying close attention to my own processes.

Profound technological and social changes require designers to be fluent in a variety of approaches to solving problems. As audiences diversify and as information is increasingly accessed and communities shaped by digital means, designers must be able to confront the interconnectedness of problems and society. Methodologies and processes can aid in the understanding of the connections and relationships.

This book demonstrates and explains how design is shaped by research methodologies and processes as applied to understanding audiences, organizing and using content, developing strategies, and defining purposes. To do this, it emphasizes not only client-associated and user-centered work but also non-client-associated, self-generated work, making a case for the latter as a way of informing the former.

The discussion begins with a section on problem seeking and solving presented as the underlying framework. Chapter 1 takes a broad look at research and introduces the book's issues, while Chapter 5 culminates the discussion through an in-depth focus on select designers' methodologies and processes. Chapters 2 through 4 cover the basics of how research methodologies and processes are applied (interpreting), function (targeting), and execution (creating).

Some methodologies and processes are common to all human activity and are used subconsciously, while others require study, practice, and reflection to be used effectively.

Many graphic design methodologies and processes originate or are widely used in other disciplines. For example, Gestalt psychology (the study of how humans perceive form) is the domain of psychology but applied in symbol design. Ethnography research (the study of user patterns) is the domain of anthropology but commonly employed in web design. These methodologies, along with others explored in this book, contribute to defining design as a discipline.

This book will help you:

· Recognize, interpret, and articulate the primary graphic design research methodologies and processes

· Understand, develop, and assess your own methodologies and processes

· Design more strategically, critically, collaboratively, ethically, and creatively for specific audiences, contexts, and responses

Even the best methodology and process cannot ensure good design. Success still depends on your ability to be engaged, to effectively draw from your experience, and to rely on your intuition and innate abilities. Like a well-designed and appropriately used grid, a methodology provides guidance through its conceptual framework.

John Bowers Introduction to Graphic Design Methodologies and Processes

Problem Seeking and Solving

0.1
Planet Earth

Problem Seeking
Increasingly used in education, problem seeking describes non-client-associated, often community-based engagement of an issue (such as sustainability) with an undetermined end form (e.g., from an informational poster to a neighborhood recycling program).

Problem Solving
Problem solving is the cognitive process of engaging an issue or set of conditions for the purpose of transforming it.

Humans by nature are seekers of meaning and solvers of problems. We are in a constant search to improve our lives and those of others, and to exercise a degree of control over our interactions and experiences. We have the capacity for reasoning and logical thinking, and thus can make associations, comparisons, and judgments that aid this search.

In the broadest sense, this describes problem solving. A problem in this context is viewed as a challenge and an opportunity, not something to avoid. It is a question raised for consideration and a solution.

Problem Seeking and Solving

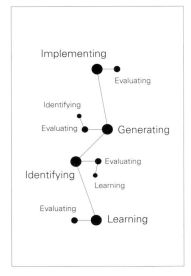

0.2
Branching
approach

A solution is found
by revisiting a
problem's conditions.

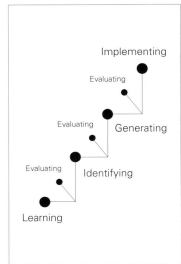

0.3
Linear
approach

A solution is
created through
sequential development.

Problem-Solving Phases
The basic problem-solving
phases of learning, identifying,
generating, and implementing
can be labeled in different ways.

· Discover
· Invent
· Launch
· Extend
(Doblin Group)

· Look
· Learn
· Ask
· Try
(IDEO)

Four basic problem-solving phases are learning,
identifying, generating, and implementing. These phases
can branch in different directions or be linear or branching—
or a combination. Most graphic design activity moves
in a branching manner; rarely is the path linear.
Reflection, analysis, and evaluation occur at every step.

The four problem-solving phases overlap and may
be repeated. Moving backwards is as common as moving
forward. The goal is to consider carefully the problem at
hand and not reach a solution prematurely.

Problem Seeking and Solving

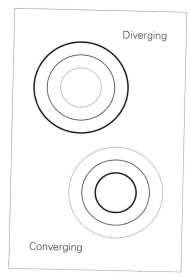

0.4
Divergent and
convergent thinking

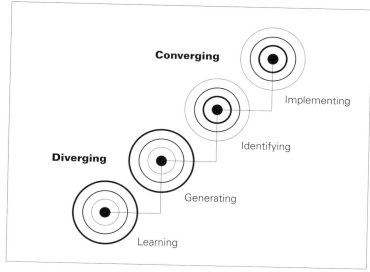

0.5
Divergent and
convergent thinking and
problem solving

Divergent thinking (discovering, predicting,
identifying, and considering) blends with
convergent thinking (prioritizing, generating,
refining, and making) during the design process.

The problem-solving process diverges and converges,
expands and contracts. Divergence is the process
of identifying, creating, and developing multiple ways
of solving a problem. Convergence is the process of
selecting and developing concepts from the previous step's
multiple pursuits.

In the learning phase, the process diverges and expands
as information is gathered, then contracts as information is
analyzed in the identifying phase. The process then again
expands in the generating phase as multiple concepts
are developed, and contracts in the evaluating phase, in
which a single concept is refined, chosen, and implemented.
Although each phase has its unique aspects, they can overlap.

Problem Seeking and Solving

0.6
Photographs of
Eames Furniture Collection Kiosk, 2003
John Bowers

In the initial phase, primary
information about the project
was sought.

Read more about this in
Chapters 2 and 5.

· Learning

Learning about the conditions that underlie and define
a problem is the first step to solving it. This phase is largely
conducted with the client and members of a design team.
Activities include the following:

· Talking and listening to the client
· Reading about the subject
· Visiting a physical space
· Talking with others informally
· Assembling a design team
· Reviewing and presenting information gathered

Problem Seeking and Solving

Project Brief

· Problem Summary
· Goals and Strategy
· Target Audience

· Deliverables
· Deadlines
· Resources and Participants

· Feedback Paths
· Evaluation Methods

4.
What is the desired user experience for each? (behaviors/actions) ~the~
To experience the simplicity, playfulness and connected nature of Eames work; to access information in individual and multiple ways; ~to compare and contrast work~
5.
What were the project parameters or constraints you were working within?
(integration with existing site, technology requirements, limited budget, etc.)
The project was done pro-bono, there was no budget. No digital or print experience (e.g.: catalog) documenting and cataloging collection, previously existed.
6.
What process and/or methodologies did your team use during the project?
(usability research, wireframes, etc.) ~and there was no budget!~
> Usability:
Because the project was pro-bono it was not subject to formal/commercial usability testing. Usabilty was assessed by students and colleagues (experienced programmers and designers) at the University of Arizona Treistman Center for New Media. Audience navigational abilities determined through experience with audience (working with colleagues and teaching students).
> Process/Methodology:
— Conceptualization ~at OSU~
Visual Audit/Positioning Matrixes
Functionality Listing
Wireframe
Architecture/Interface
Production (Photoshop/Flash)

0.7
Project brief components

0.8
Conceptualization for
Eames Furniture Collection Kiosk, 2003
John Bowers

A project brief was written that outlined the project's components and objectives.

Read more about this in Chapters 3 and 5.

· Identifying

Identifying the purpose of a project and its different parts, sensibly grouping the parts, and prioritizing them constitute the next step. Goals are established and an underlying concept developed. Activities include the following:

· Interviewing select members of the targeted audience
· Making visual audits of entity and peer groups
· Creating positioning matrices
· Writing a design brief
· Writing, receiving, organizing, and prioritizing content
· Reviewing and presenting information gathered

Problem Seeking and Solving

John Bowers Introduction to Graphic Design Methodologies and Processes

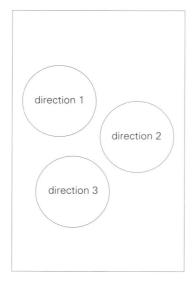

0.9
Direction generation

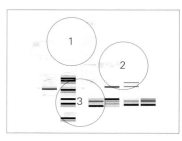

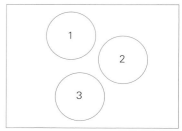

0.10
Ideation
Eames Furniture Collection Kiosk, 2003
John Bowers

Read more about this in
Chapters 4 and 5.

· Generating

Generating ideas that could become possible solutions
comes next. The goal at this point is to give form to a concept.
The visual and verbal components are established, and
multiple visual expressions (directions) on a single concept
are created, from which a single direction is chosen.
Activities include the following:

· Making thinking maps and visualization matrices
· Generating attribute lists and concept statements
· Creating off-computer sketches, images, and material studies
· Creating on-computer color, font, grid, and
typography studies
· Doing on-computer design iterations
· Reviewing and presenting work

Problem Seeking and Solving

0.11
Pages from
Eames Furniture Collection Kiosk, 2003
John Bowers

A single direction was chosen and refined.

Read more about this in
Chapters 4 and 5.

· Implementing

Implementing and evaluating a solution is the final step.
While refinement and evaluation of the solution to meet
the project's goals take place throughout the design
process, they culminate here and hopefully reinforce earlier
decisions. An internal assessment may be done to better
understand studio practices. Activities include the following:

· Conducting focus group testing
· Holding usability testing
· Seeking informal feedback
· Placing work in context
· Doing project assessment
· Reviewing work

John Bowers Introduction to Graphic Design Methodologies and Processes

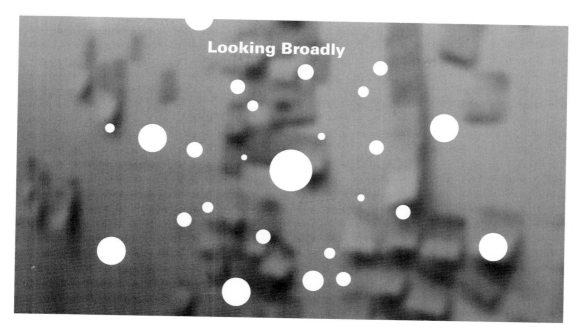

Looking Broadly

Concepts

Researching
Information
Forms
Approaches
Methodologies
Processes

This chapter introduces research methodologies and creative processes.

Looking Broadly

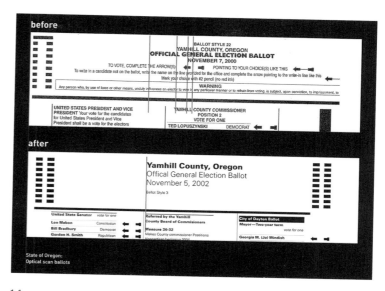

1.1
Voter ballot, 2002
Client: Oregon Election Commission
Gretchen Schulfer

The redesign of a voter ballot resulted in a clearer presentation of choices and party affiliations, more accurate selections, and quicker tabulations.

Research
In the broadest sense, research is the search for knowledge and advancement in a deliberate and engaged, if not systematic, manner.

Epistemology
This branch of philosophy studies knowledge, questioning what it is and how it is acquired.

Every day we use a variety of methods and processes to accomplish daily tasks and ensure desired results. At the grocery store, for example, we may carry a list of needed items, go through the aisles in a chosen order, and check our receipts on the way out. Such steps are led by a point of view, guided by experience, and often applied subconsciously.

Similar to developing routines and approaches that help us in our everyday lives, becoming familiar with and fluent in graphic design methods and processes can help us solve design problems. Each design problem is unique, yet related to other visual systems and to society at large. Competency in a range of approaches is required to inspire viewers and users effectively and to guide their responses.

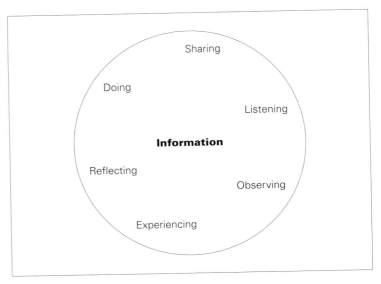

1.2
Predominant
ways of gathering
information

Information is gathered through our senses, analyzed through cognitive processes such as communication, learning, and reasoning, and shaped by our experiences, needs, and desires. Information acquisition can be actively sought or passively absorbed.

Learning by Doing
This theory refers to gaining knowledge through practice, by repeating a set or sets of actions to improve the outcome over time.

Gathering information and making sense of it are critical to leading a fulfilled life. Ways of gaining information can be organized into two primary groups.

· Experiencing, Doing, and Sharing

This grouping describes learning from the accumulation of direct experience of participating and doing, including sharing knowledge with others. Traveling to a new place and telling stories about your experiences is one example.

· Observing, Listening, and Reflecting

This grouping describes an active search for knowledge outside your immediate experiences, analyzing that knowledge, and perhaps testing it. Reading about a place where you've never been and discussing it with others who have been there is one example.

Looking Broadly Forms

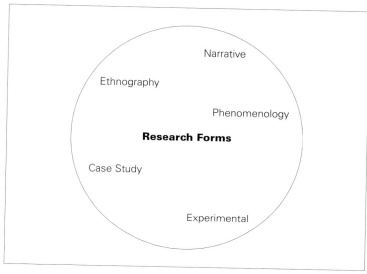

1.3
IDEO Method Cards, 2003
IDEO

1.4
Research forms

Many graphic design activities employ multiple research forms. IDEO method cards blend ethnographic and narrative research to target audience preferences and trends.

Research Forms
Dominant research forms used in graphic design include the following:

· Case study (description and analysis of an activity)
· Ethnography (interpretation of a cultural group)
· Experimental (experimentation with select variables)
· Narrative (understanding individual experiences)
· Phenomenology (understanding the essence of experiences)

Given the complexity of contemporary design problems, research forms are often applied in combination.

· Ethnography

Employed in advertising and some forms of persuasive graphic design such as identity design, ethnography involves the observation of a cultural group and analysis and interpretation of the group's patterns.

· Experimental

This form of research is based on experimentation with select variables such as font size or weight. It is used throughout virtually all design activities.

John Bowers Introduction to Graphic Design Methodologies and Processes

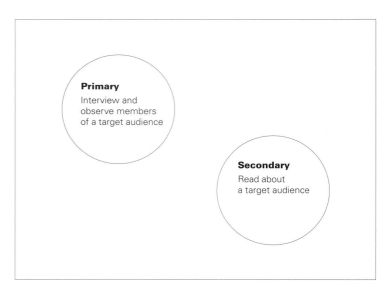

1.5
Primary and secondary approaches

" We see the development
of research in design to be
a combination of two
aspects: the search for
existing knowledge
developed by other
disciplines and the creation
of new knowledge.
By accessing the knowledge
base of other disciplines
such as sociology,
psychology, anthropology,
and education, research
in design can find a way to
its own development." [1]

Sharon Helmer Poggenpohl
Professor,
Hong Kong Polytechnique
University

Information can be acquired in a multitude of ways, including through primary and secondary research.

· Primary

Primary research is used to find new information. The majority of graphic design activity falls into this category, as designers typically work directly with clients (and target audiences) to identify and analyze problems.

· Secondary

Secondary research refers to the analysis of existing information. Often used in combination with primary research, it is common in identity and interaction design, activities that require a thorough understanding of audience demographics and abilities.

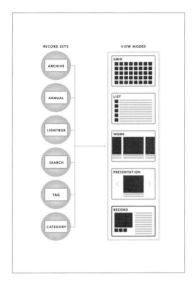

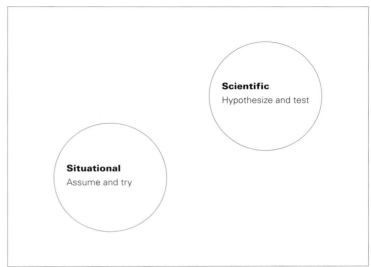

1.6
Website user interface study, 2010
Client: AIGA
Second Story Interactive Studios

1.7
Scientific
and situational
approaches

The AIGA website user interface study was a combination
of both approaches. Projections about user navigational
abilities led the project and were later tested though direct
observation of users interacting with the website.

Bloom's Taxonomy
Benjamin S. Bloom, a renowned
educational psychologist,
developed the following list of
sequential cognitive skills
necessary for critical thinking.
Acquiring knowledge is the
starting point for creating
informed and meaningful design.

· Knowledge
· Comprehension
· Application
· Analysis
· Synthesis
· Evaluation

Situational experience and scientific research are but two
approaches to gathering and forming useful knowledge.

· Situational

Situational knowledge is based on a simple assumption
about a situation (e.g., to continue reading this book, you'll
need to turn the page). It is shaped by experience and
cultural conventions (e.g., in the West we read a book from
front to back).

· Scientific

Scientific knowledge is driven by observations and
hypotheses, which are derived from experiments
and logical deductions. These lead to experiments and
tests, which are based on the collection of measurable
data and conducted to prove a hypothesis.

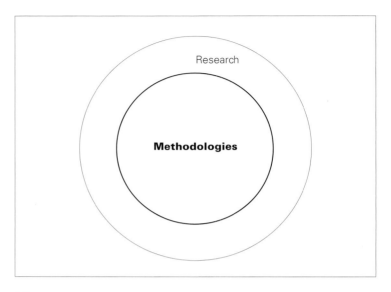

1.8
Relationship of research and methodology

Methodology
A methodology is a set
of procedures for inquiry into
a particular discipline.

Proprietary Methodology
A proprietary methodology
is possessed, owned, or held
exclusively (often through
legal protection) by an individual
or organization.

At the core of research are methodologies. These are
collections of theories, beliefs, concepts or ideas,
and philosophical assumptions upon which an approach
is based.

A research methodology describes how to undertake
an investigation and how to evaluate the results.
In graphic design, it could consist of a stated purpose,
a process, assumptions about the content or audience,
and desired responses.

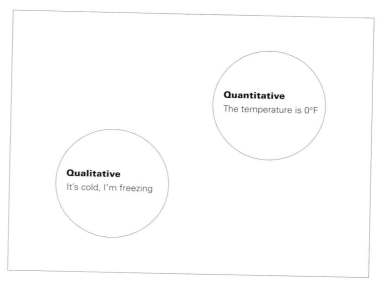

1.9
Qualitative and quantitative
research methodologies

Research Plans
As the initial step in a research
investigation, a research plan
addresses four basic questions.

· What is the goal?
· What methods will be used?
· What resources are needed?
· What are the benefits?

Methodologies break down into four basic categories that
describe their processes, outcomes, and evaluative
approaches: qualitative, quantitative, deductive, and inductive.

· Qualitative

Qualitative research is common in the humanities, including
the fine arts. In these disciplines information is largely
created through direct action and not through the acquisition
or application of facts. Qualitative research includes
some forms of narrative and experimental research methods.
Evaluation of the results is predominantly subjective.

· Quantitative

Common in the social sciences, quantitative research is
based on the collection of data (including facts and statistics)
through questionnaires, interviews, and other forms of
observational and participatory methods.

Looking Broadly Methodologies

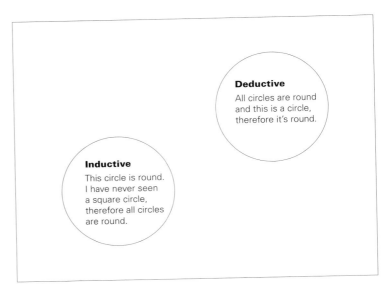

1.10
Deductive and inductive reasoning

Logic
Logic is the study of reasoning.

Intelligences
Psychologist Howard Gardner
lists the intelligence types
of humans. Those that pertain to
graphic design activity include:

· Verbal-linguistic
· Logical-mathematical
· Visual-spatial
· Intrapersonal
· Interpersonal

· Deductive

A deductive reasoning approach begins with a broad and
general statement or belief that is used as the basis for
reaching a specific conclusion. The beginning and ending
items are related by an object or event.

· Inductive

Inductive reasoning begins with observations about a
specific event, activity, or object. It then uses this as
the basis for developing a general conclusion that can
be applied to all like events, activities, or objects.

Most graphic design activity employs deductive reasoning,
in which the activity begins with the creation of many
possible solutions to a problem that are then narrowed
down to a single solution.

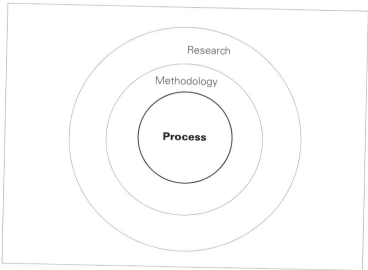

1.11
Conceptualization process
workshop
Umeå Institute of Design, 2010

1.12
Research, methodology, and
process relationship

The Post-it process was used to easily
identify, organize, and prioritize content.

Process
Process refers to the steps
or procedures that constitute a
research activity.

Processes are embedded in and drive methodologies.
They can be sequential and repeatable, or random and
difficult to reproduce.

Often, the same problem can be solved through any number
of processes to achieve an effective solution. While the
process for most graphic design activity is similar (e.g.,
rough ideas to refined solutions), each person has a unique
perspective and set of work habits, and applies this basic
process differently.

Graphic design processes are becoming increasingly
collaborative and participatory, and take into account a
work's physical environment and social interactions.

John Bowers Introduction to Graphic Design Methodologies and Processes

2

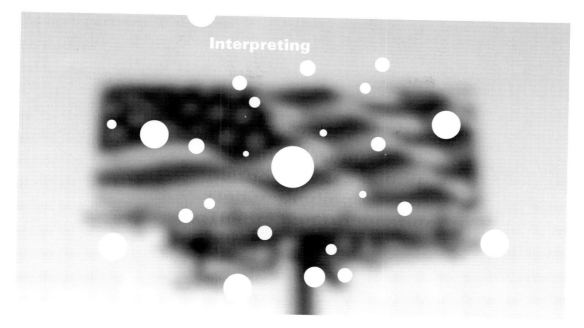

Interpreting

Concepts

Sending and Receiving
Communication
Lenses
Theory
Contemporary Theorists
Semiotic Theory
Deconstruction and Relational Theory

Reading
Knowledge Domains
Value Assessment
Process
Textuality

This chapter examines the theories, processes, and social or cultural influences that shape how messages are sent, received, and interpreted.

Interpreting Messages

For a closer look, see Chapter 5

2.1
Front and back cover of
Intelligent Design: Creating an Evolved Red vs. Blue State of Mind, 2005
Client and Design: Thirst Studio

Through a computer program, this work translates each word of the Book of Genesis into a Coke or Pepsi can as commentary on consumption and religion.

"Every decision is connected to another and every action causes reactions that ripple throughout all aspects of our culture and environment." [2]

Meredith Davis
Professor, Graduate
Program Director, and
Head of the interdisciplinary PhD
in Design program,
North Carolina State University

Our ability to send messages that prompt desired responses and to critically interpret the messages received is vital in the search for meaning.

The interpretation of messages, whether symbolic, abstract, or literal, is an everyday process that invokes our unique backgrounds, values, beliefs, and morals. These and other factors shape our responses to messages and our expectations of their implied promises.

Understanding the contemporary theories and methodologies that guide the creation and dissemination of messages is helpful in informed communication.

Interpreting Communication

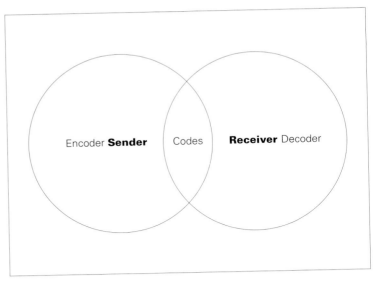

Encoder **Sender**   Codes   **Receiver** Decoder

2.2
Communication model

Codes are transferred in the communication process.

Encoding
Encoding is the process of creating forms with signals and cues that can guide a response.

Codes
Codes are symbols that lead to interpretations, such as those for gender roles. They may be created through the use of color to reinforce stereotypes, e.g., pink for girls, blue for boys, or suggest new viewpoints.

Decoding
Decoding is the process of analyzing a message and determining its meaning. Decoding is influenced by the physical location and cultural context of a message, as well as the receiver's decoding abilities and familiarity with the message and its visual language.

Communication occurs via a sender, receiver, form or medium, and message. Embedded in messages are codes from the sender that transfer information (ideas, thoughts, opinions, etc.).

The receiver may interpret the codes through the help of cues and signals. In interactive form, cues and signals can be conveyed visually and audibly, such as by a button that changes color and makes a sound when pressed. In print form, cues and signals may be focal points and suggested reading orders, such as top to bottom and left to right.

Both the sender and the receiver must understand the language employed in the communication process for the meaning to be fully gained.

Interpreting Lenses

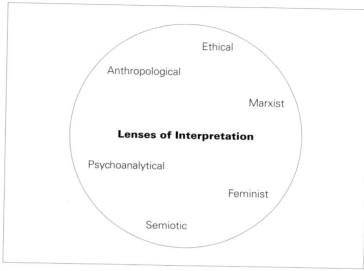

2.3
Billboard
Portland, Oregon, 2001

2.4
Lenses of interpretation

Lenses of interpretation can be employed
individually or in combination.

Lenses
The dominant lenses of
interpretation applied in graphic
design messages include
the following:

· Anthropological (expression
of a ritual or place)
· Ethical (social or cultural
implications)
· Feminist (role in supporting
equality for women
and humankind at large)
· Marxist (economic conditions
under which a message is
created and the goals it supports)
· Psychoanalytical (value and
meaning of a viewer's experience)
· Semiotic (purpose of a
message and ability to function
in its context)

The many lenses or perspectives through which a visual
message can be created and interpreted are influenced
by belief systems, culture, literacy, motives, and values.
Whether consciously or subconsciously, we employ
some or all of these elements when deriving meaning
from a message.

Empathy for others and appreciation of other perspectives
are important qualities to possess. Designers must
often reconcile multiple and conflicting points of view
on a single topic from the audience, the client, or even
within themselves.

Interpreting Theory

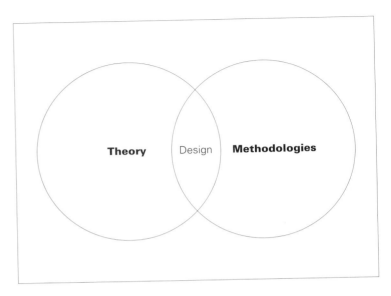

2.5
Relationship of theory and methodologies

Theory
Theory refers to groupings of
ideas that seek to explain a
phenomenon, guide investigation,
or form interpretation.

Theory serves as a guide to searching, planning,
explaining, interpreting, and understanding. It is the basis
of any systematic investigation. Theory can help clarify
problems and ideas, aid in the interpretation of data
and experiences, and suggest methods by which a problem
can be solved.

Through application, theories are proven usable
or unusable, true or false, repeatable or not repeatable.
Qualitative investigations, common in graphic design,
generally develop theories as they proceed.
These investigations can also be rooted in a theory
that spans many disciplines, such as semiotic theory.

Modernism Late 1890s to present

Structuralism
Examination of structural components and relationships that yield meaning
Ferdinand de Saussure

Semiotics
Examination of signs (signifiers) and the process of determining meaning
Roland Barthes

Post-Modernism 1960s to present

Post-Structuralism
Examination of embedded codes as a way of expanding interpretation
Michel Foucault

Deconstruction
Examination of embedded opposites as a way of deriving multiple meanings
Jacques Derrida

Relational
Examination of context and participation as a way of guiding interpretation
Nicolas Bourriaud

2.6
(Top) Cover for *Dada Painters*, 1951
Paul Rand
(Bottom) Page spread from *VAS*, 2003
Stephen Farrell

2.7
Select contemporary thought

Contemporary graphic design is explained, in part, through the examination of theory in linguistics, philosophy, literature, and anthropology.

Audience
Audience refers to the receiver of a message. An audience can be targeted or open-ended, narrow or broad, familiar or unfamiliar (with content or content navigational devices such as a website interface), and treated as passive observers or active participants.

Graphic design is influenced by and employs modernist and post-modernist theories. Each theory has distinguishing features and comprises thought from many disciplines, particularly in the humanities. While post-modernist work is largely characterized by the use of more participatory methodologies including ethnographic research, the lines between the two theories are often blurred.

Interpreting Semiotic Theory

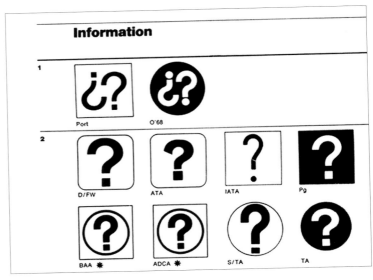

2.8
Global information study,
1993

A study of global symbols evaluated through semiotic theory.

Representation
Representation is created through aspects of signs. In this context, a sign is a visual concept, not necessarily a physical sign.

· Symbols (meaning is culturally agreed upon, such as the letter i and the question mark)
· Icons (meaning is derived from resemblance to an object, such as a pointing hand to indicate help)
· Indexes (meaning is derived through reasoning and association, such as a question mark beside a person's desk to indicate available assistance)

Semiotic theory, a branch of linguistics that examines the function and meaning of signs, has three aspects that aid in the development and evaluation of visual messages.

· Syntactic

In this aspect, the formal relationships among a form's elements or among related forms are examined to determine if they are unified.

· Semantic

In this aspect, the relationship between a form and its intended meaning is examined to determine if its message is effectively expressed.

· Pragmatic

In this aspect, the form is examined in its context to determine if its message is understandable.

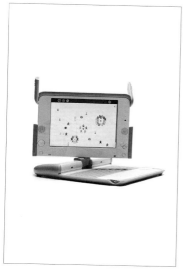

2.9
The $100 computer, 2006
MIT Media Lab

2.10
Detail from
VAS, 2002
Stephen Farrell

The $100 hand-cranked computer uses the Linux open source operating system, which allows for collaborative development and free usage. Farrell's work expands the use of typography as a communicative device.

Deconstruction and relational theory are two important influences on contemporary graphic design.

· Deconstruction

Work based on this approach tends to embrace nonlinear reading orders and the viewer as participant in creating a work's narrative. Experimental and expressive typography are often based on deconstruction.

· Relational Theory

Largely based on the writings of Bourriaud, relational theory examines a work's context and the ways a design can facilitate social interactions and empowerment. It examines and relates messages and forms to viewers and users in their social and physical context. Open source programming and website customization are two examples of relational theory in use.

Interpreting Content

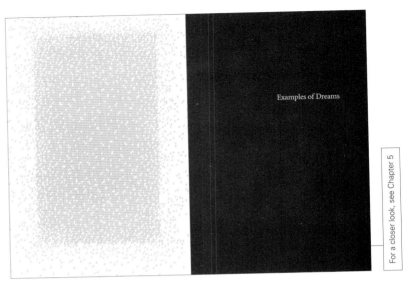

For a closer look, see Chapter 5

Examples of Dreams

2.11
Page from
To Sleep, Perchance to Dream, 2008
Studio A

This book explores the knowledge domain of sleep, visualizing its stages and mystery through progressive imagery.

Knowledge Domain
A knowledge domain refers to a field of knowledge.

Text and images about a knowledge domain such as a birthday can be presented through these groupings:

· Events

An event is a setting or a place in which objects and activities connect.

· Objects

Using a birthday party example, objects can include a cake, candles, and gifts.

· Activities

Activities in this context refer to the plans or actions that relate to the objects supporting an event. For example, during a birthday party (event), candles (objects) are placed on a cake and blown out (activity) in celebration.

Interpreting Value Assessment

2.12
Common assessments

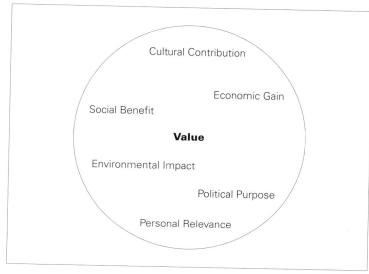

2.13
Assessment criteria

Value can be intrinsic (originating in an object, belonging to its essential nature) or instrumental (serving as a means, agent, or tool).

Critical Thinking
The term critical thinking comes from the Greek word *kriterion*, which means a position from which to make a judgment. Critical thinking describes thinking that is active and engaged. It examines credibility, biases, accuracy, strengths, relevance of information, questions, and assumptions.

As the number of messages increases, the need to assess their value increases accordingly. Two primary value categories can be used in this assessment.

· Point of View

The points of view held by various design participants (designer, client, audience) influence assessment through the application of personal experiences, needs, and values.

· Context

The physical location or virtual environment of a message and the effect of time can heighten or diminish a message's value. For example, the letter X on a sidewalk may designate an excavation site for a public utility; on a greeting card it may represent a kiss and an expression of affection (e.g., XOXO); and on a shopping list it may indicate that an item was found.

Interpreting Process

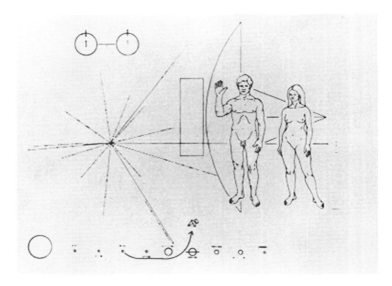

2.14
Plaque aboard Pioneer 10,
launched March 2, 1972
Frank Drake, Carl Sagan, and
Linda Sagan, designers

This plaque uses symbols to convey
information about Earth, including its
position in the solar system.

Visual Literacy
Visual literacy is the ability to
interpret, evaluate, and derive
meaning from images.

Visual Language
Visual language refers to a
message's visual elements, their
arrangement and emphasis,
and what they reference. It is
a combination of style, taste,
aesthetics, and strategy.

Cues
Cues are visual identifiers
that signal an action or help
form an interpretation.
Underlined text on a website,
for example, is a cue indicating
that the text is a clickable link.

Reading images—photographs, drawings, charts, maps,
symbols, etc.—refers to the process of decoding an image,
interpreting it, and deriving its meaning. It is an acquired
skill that involves the ability to:

· Engage the visual language being used
· Identify and decode embedded codes
· Assess and synthesize the information presented
· Assign value to the message

Interpreting Textuality

2.15
Advertisement, 1996
Wieden and Kennedy
Eugene Richards, photographer

2.16
Advertisement, 1992
Concept: O. Toscani
United Colors of Bennetton

The cowboy is often used to connote masculinity and independence. Imagery presenting personal narratives can be used to gain affinity and loyalty.

Denotation and Connotation
Denotation refers to the physical appearance of an object: a square is a shape with four equal sides. Connotation refers to an interpretation of an object: a square can suggest neutrality or stability.

Signs
A sign is an image, symbol, sound, or word (signifier) that indicates a meaning (signified).

Metaphors
Metaphors use words or images to suggest a likeness to another object or concept.

An image can be read literally, textually, and/or intertextually.

· Literal

Literal reading examines formal visual elements such as colors, their associations, and interactions.

· Textual

Textual reading refers to the placement of an image within a story or text and can include the examination of how an image supports a written narrative or expresses a visual narrative.

· Intertextual

Intertextual reading refers to how an image references other images, styles, traditions, or events. This may include appropriation of an image's role in supporting a ritual.

25

John Bowers Introduction to Graphic Design Methodologies and Processes

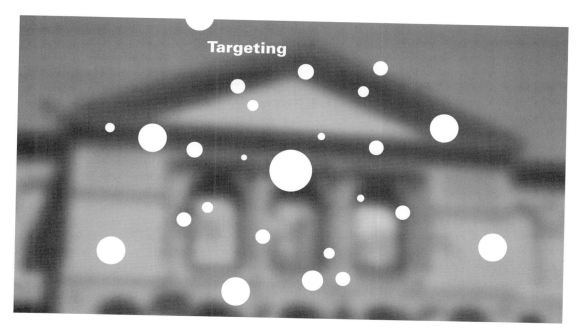

Targeting

Concepts

Strategizing
Planning
Strategy
Goals
Response
Decision Making

Gathering
Participation
Ethnography
Projections
Observation

Making
Visual Audits
Positioning Statements
Positioning Matrices

Sharing
Assessment
Evaluation

This chapter explores methodologies and processes of understanding audiences and targeting messages to achieve specific responses.

Targeting Audiences and Responses

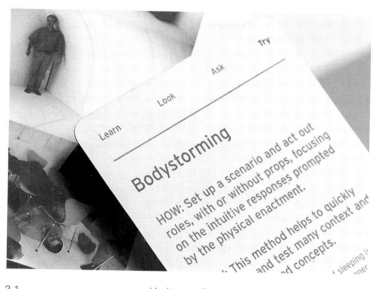

3.1
Front and back of
IDEO Method Cards, 2003
IDEO

Understanding audiences is vital in creating effective messages for them. Method cards can be used in focus group settings to help develop ideas and strategies.

"**Designers need to understand the sense and sensibility differences of cultures, their peoples' communication needs and value declarations, and the barriers that hinder facilitation. Insight gleaned therein provides designers with concrete data for the formation of concepts, plans, and schemes to solve visual communication problems for a multi-faceted, multi-religious, multi-layered and multi-ethnic world community.**" [3]

Dietmar Winkler
Professor Emeritus,
Visual Design Department
University of Massachusetts,
Dartmouth

Graphic design messages target audiences to elicit specific responses. For instance, a poster might both inform and enlighten the viewers of an exhibition, while an advertisement might persuade and encourage consumers to purchase a product.

To achieve a message's response goals, identifying and understanding the audience are critical and involve planning, audience observation and analysis, and strategy building. Methodologies and processes aid in the creation and evaluation of effective and engaging messages.

Analyzing similar messages as well as understanding your role as designer is also important. As the designer of a message, you and your client may not be the audience; your personal design tastes and methodology preference may not be applicable.

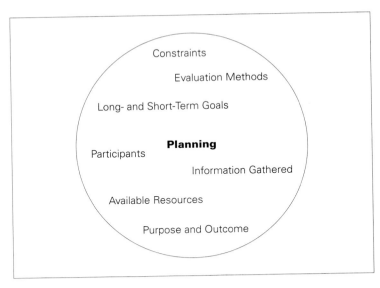

Constraints

Evaluation Methods

Long- and Short-Term Goals

Planning

Participants

Information Gathered

Available Resources

Purpose and Outcome

3.2
Planning components

Planning involves practical and abstract components, any of which may be dominant. Primary components include determining objectives and developing options.

Planning is the process of selecting, analyzing, and organizing activities required to achieve a goal.

Planning helps clarify and focus a project. It also provides a framework for assessing the results: Did the plan work and can it be used again? A plan determines and prioritizes what needs to be done, in what order, by whom, and when. It can help you determine objectives and develop options, including deadlines, a budget, audience, location, and outcomes.

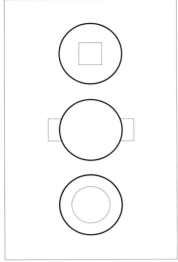

Available Resources

Long-and Short-Term Goals

Strategy

Relation to Peers

Methodologies and Processes

Growth Areas

3.3
U.S.–proposed table arrangements for the U.S.–North Vietnam peace talks, 1968

3.4
Strategy components

Negotiation power was the goal in the design of the U.S.–North Vietnam peace table. A simple circular table was ultimately agreed upon.

The basic components of strategy are apparent in games (players and boundaries), sports (offense and defense), and war (tactics and surprise).

Strategic planning targets specific outcomes in a competitive market. It typically includes short- and long-term plans for which activities can be reviewed for future projects.

A mission and vision statement can help develop strategies. The end result of a strategy can range from strictly commercial, such as increasing a company's profits, to humanitarian, such as increasing donations for a cause.

These basic questions may be asked about an entity during the strategic planning process:

· What are our core values?
· What are others doing?
· Where do we want to be, and how do we get there?

3.5
Goal-setting components

Primary goals are defined by vision, information, and the desired outcome.

Goals are statements of desires, needs, and vision. Within goals are objectives—specific activities required to achieve the goals. Whereas goals are general intentions, objectives are precise, concrete, and able to be benchmarked and validated.

To achieve a goal, you need to determine what resources, skills, and knowledge are necessary. Good planning is required, along with effective coordination of team members and engaged design.

A goal can be directed toward the making of profit, brand loyalty, publicity, or recognition, or it can simply be for experimentation, which in turn can lead to profit or be part of a public service.

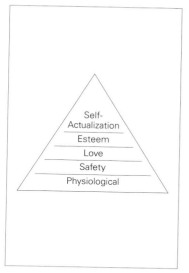

3.6
Maslow's hierarchy of needs

3.7
Identity symbol, 1971
Client: Nike
Carolyn Davidson, designer

The Nike symbol alludes to speed and magical power to target the human desire of achievement.

Maslow's Hierarchy of Needs

In 1934, psychologist Abraham Maslow created a representation of human needs:

· Self-actualization (creativity)
· Esteem (respect and achievement)
· Love (belonging and intimacy)
· Safety (income and relationships)
· Physiological (food and shelter)

A response is a reaction to a stimulus. A stimulus might be an informative poster about voting, for example, with the viewer's response leading to voting a certain way, reflecting on a political position, or simply gaining information about a voting procedure.

To achieve such responses, basic needs and desires must be targeted. In branding, visual identities create expectations and imply value about a service or product, which can lead to viewer perception of a brand and in turn a response.

In advertising, messages serve as stimuli, seeking the purchase of products as a result, with repeated and high-volume purchases as goals.

3.8
Decision-making
components

The primary components influencing individual and
group decision making are interrelated.

Collaboration
Collaboration is the process
of sharing and working with
others toward a common goal.
Effective collaboration is
based on:

· Ability to accept
  a participatory role
· Commitment to the process
· Effective communication
· Empathy and respect for others
· Good listening skills

Decision making is the process of weighing and choosing
options. Graphic design work employs a variety of decision-
making methods, including intuition (relying on a hunch),
chance (accidental discoveries), deference (allowing someone
else to decide), experience, and analysis (researching and
creating alternatives from which to choose).

In designer-client relationships, decisions are typically made
from the top down (e.g., the client conveys ideas to the design
director, who guides the designer) and/or laterally (the client,
design director, and designer work together as equals).
When multiple participants share in the decision-making
process, it is important to first decide whether the decision
will be reached by consensus or another method.

The way decisions are made can have a significant influence
on a project's final outcome. While "design by committee"
is largely viewed as ineffective, encouraging the participation
of multiple voices can often enrich the process.

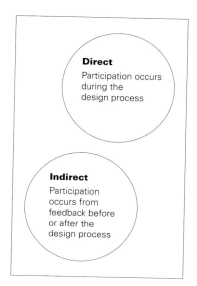

3.9
Participation types

3.10
Do It Yourself exhibition, 2006
Ellen Lupton, curator

Participation can be direct and/or indirect.
In this DIY exhibition, attendees became direct
participants by writing and posting messages
and found images.

Do It Yourself (DIY)
DIY is a movement in which
individuals with little or
no training create, improve,
and invent without the direct
help of professionals.

Participation
Participation is a process through
which individuals and groups
make decisions by sharing
control, access to resources,
and goal setting, as well as
responsibility and accountability
for the end result. Important
considerations guiding the
process include:

· Who is allowed to participate?
· How do they participate?
· Is participation meaningful?
· Is participation voluntary?

Messages can be developed through direct or indirect
participation. Through participation, individuals and
communities influence and share control. Forms may also
foster participation. Websites, for instance, are participatory
forms; while access to the content is guided by the design,
users control what will be sought and in what order.

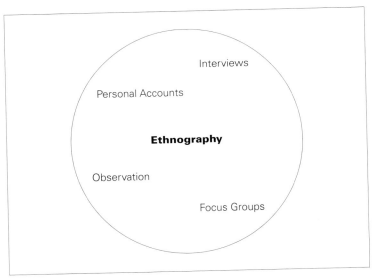

3.11
Ethnography methods

Ethnography involves a variety of information-gathering methods and personal qualities.

Ethnography

Ethnography is a method of research that observes, documents, and analyzes people interacting with designed objects and experiences in normal, everyday situations. This research can provide designers with the information to improve their investigations.

Human-Centered Design

Human-centered design is based on an understanding of user patterns and abilities. It focuses on designing objects and interactions that are rooted in observed experiences.

Learning about your audience is important to creating effective messages and experiences. Ethnographic research is used in many disciplines, including graphic design. It is a direct form of observation and information gathering. Concerned with the link between culture and behavior, it allows for a better understanding of a market, which in turns aids strategic development.

A systematic and deliberate process, ethnography can reveal individual habits, routines, and values, and larger trends and patterns, confirming or denying what a designer already knows intuitively.

Such study can reveal the influence of design on viewers and, in particular, brand identity, including how a brand can create perceptions and build loyalty. This can lead to design that better targets the intended audience and elicits the response desired by the creator.

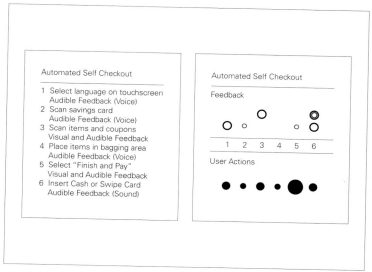

3.12
Persona
John DeVylder

3.13
Flowchart

A flowchart can plan the visual and audible experience
and illustrate how users can move through content.

Persona
A persona is a fictional narrative
about a representative member
of a target audience. It is written
as an aid to understanding an
audience's profile.

Flowcharts
A flowchart is a diagram that
shows the decision-making
process of a person involved
in a particular activity, such
as shopping or interacting with
digital media.

Predicting how audiences will respond to messages or
move through content can be helpful in effectively targeting
them. Personas and flowcharts are two predictive approaches
that use narrative to suggest what and how viewers seek.
This is particularly useful in web design, where the navigation
must guide user interactions.

Personas and flowcharts are useful in understanding an
audience's needs, patterns, buying habits, and preferences.
Personas are particularly useful in the design of websites and
associated branding.

A common flowchart projection is a fictional illustration of
a consumer's path toward making a purchase. It shows a
consumer's decision-making process and the effect of stimuli
preceding a purchase.

Targeting Observation

John Bowers   Introduction to Graphic Design Methodologies and Processes

Interview Guidelines

· Respondent Demographics
· Room Setup
· Questions and Activities
· Feedback Options
· Observation Method

Question Categories

· Brand Competition
· Brand Personality

Outcomes

· Learning Buying Patterns
· Understanding User Traits

Information about an audience's perception of a given brand, message, or form can be gained in a variety of ways, including through guided, direct participation.

3.14
Sample client interview guidelines and question categories

3.15
IDEO Method Cards, 2003
IDEO

Focus Groups
A focus group is a collection of individuals assembled by a strategist. They are shown select materials about a company or organization and its visual presence, and asked questions such as:

· What is the message?
· Does this remind you of another company?
· Does it look as if it comes from the same company?
· Whom does the message target?
· Does this work positively influence you about the company?
· Does the work match your perception of the company?

In ethnographic research, select participants are observed or asked directly about their perceptions, opinions, and attitudes toward a brand (as expressed through a package or identity system) or their experience (in the form of a website, printed material, or signage). The forms of this research include:

Interviews and Observations

· Interviews with the client and target audience
· Focus groups with the target audience and others
· Direct observation of the target audience

Documentation and Analysis

· Surveys of the target audience after the message is sent
· Behavioral mapping of the target audience's interactions
· Personal stories from the target audience about their interactions and responses

Audit Areas

· Print
· Web
· Signage

· External Identity
· Internal Correspondence
· Co-Branded Material

Audit Group

· Client
· Peer Group
· Best Practice

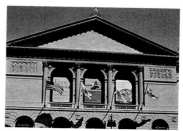

3.16
Visual audit components

3.17
Visual identity material, 2010
Art Institute of Chicago

Examples of online and printed materials
reveal an identity system's visual components,
consistency, and personality.

Visual Audit
A visual audit involves the
collection and analysis of visual
materials representing a company
or organization.

In a visual audit, print and web materials from an entity,
from members of its peer group, and from related entities
are gathered, compared, and analyzed for the use of
design to convey the organization's or company's strategy.
Consistency, visual language, emphasis, quality,
and innovation are among the evaluated characteristics.

This book provides
graphic designers with a
basic understanding
of the methodologies and
processes that can be used
to enhance their work.

3.18
Positioning statement

The positioning statement for this book identifies
the audience, the benefit, and the unique
qualities that differentiate the book from others.

Positioning Statement
A positioning statement
concisely outlines the audience
and purpose of a design project.

From the information gathered and analyzed through
audits, observation, interviews, and personas, a positioning
statement may be written to guide a project. Typically two
to three sentences in length, it outlines the values,
attributes, and goals of an entity. Commonly written by
consultants and designers together with the client, such
statements usually remain internal and are not seen by the
general public.

In brand identity work, a positioning statement can help
define an entity and position it relation to others. It can
address these questions:

· What is the brand presented?
· What does the customer expect of the brand?
· What is the outcome of the brand?

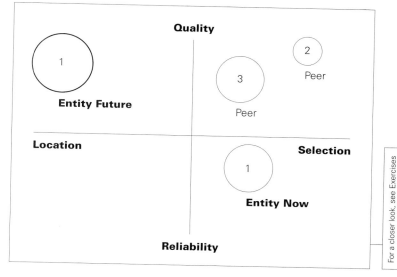

Position

· Where are you now?
· Where are others?
· Where do you want to go?

Value

· How big are you?
· How big do you want to be?

Common Aspects

· Location or Accessibility
· Quality or Status
· Inventory or Selection
· Service or Reliability

3.19
Positioning matrix considerations

3.20
Positioning matrix

In a positioning matrix, circle size can indicate values such as sales levels or recent growth.

For a closer look, see Exercises

Positioning Matrix
A positioning matrix represents the relationship of an entity to its peers. A matrix has two intersecting lines that result in four quadrants. Word opposites are placed at the ends of each intersecting line. All four words are conceptually or thematically related.

Building on a positioning statement, a positioning matrix shows differences and similarities among entities, along with growth areas, called "sweet spots." Sweet spots, which are often the open quadrants, are subjective and determined by strategy.

Matrices visually represent relationships among competitors and illustrate where they are now and might want to be in the future. Circles of different sizes within a matrix can indicate evaluative aspects, such as perceptions of value. To fully understand a market, multiple matrices can be created, each with a different focus and words.

Targeting Assessment

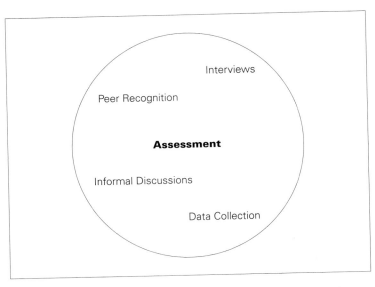

Interviews

Peer Recognition

Assessment

Informal Discussions

Data Collection

3.21
Assessment components

Assessments are made from formal and informal information gathering.

Documenting and assessing a completed project are important in developing future projects. Maintaining a record of a project's visual and verbal processes can further the quality and consistency of working processes. It can help explain how decisions were made and guide effective decision making in the future.

Self-assessment (an examination of a designer's decision-making effectiveness, research breadth and quality, and collaborative reach) aids in learning and the ability to extrapolate from one project to another.

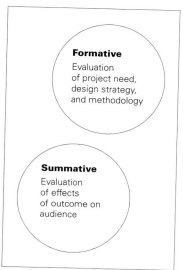

3.22
Evaluation types

USABILITY TEST QUESTIONNAIRE
AIGA design archives
Wednesday, December 16th

First name (for internal reference only):

Have you used the AIGA online archives before?

Describe how you feel about the ease or difficulty of maneuvering the overall AIGA interface. (2-3 sentences)

Describe how you feel about the ease or difficulty of using the "Breadcrumb Trail."

What is your preferred method for searching? (Search box or Filter Archives) Did anything hinder your search?

What was your favorite "View" for browsing results? (Grid view, List View, Slideshow, Detail view) Was there a "View" you had difficulty accessing?

For a closer look, see Chapter 5

3.23
Usability testing questionnaire for Design Archives Website, 2010
Client: AIGA
Second Story Interactive Studios

Website usability testing examines the user's ability to access and navigate content. User problems and satisfaction are noted in relation to specific tasks.

Evaluation
Evaluation is the systematic assessment of a work's value. Criteria may include:

· Audience Response
  Does it elicit the desired response?
· User Interaction or Viewing
  Is it accessible?
· Design Process
  Was the process effective?

Before or after a work is released, it may undergo evaluation by the client, the designer(s), and select members of the target audience. Effective evaluation is not client-centered but user- or viewer-centered; it requires openness to feedback and differing views. In interactive design, it is useful to learn about a user's choices, attention span, priorities, and preferences.

John Bowers Introduction to Graphic Design Methodologies and Processes

Concepts

Approaching
Components
Emotion
Intuition
Methodical

Organizing
Conceptualizing with Writing
Questions and Assumptions

Conceptualizing
Thinking Maps
Visualizing Matrices
Prioritizing Content
Planning and Diagramming

Making
Visualizing
Emphasizing
Documenting
Storytelling

This chapter explores a range of practical methodologies and processes for creating targeted visual messages.

Creating Visual Messages

For a closer look, see Chapter 5

4.1
Yellow Book, 2004
Michelle Bowers

Found imagery is glued into discarded library books to create visual narratives that are juxtaposed with and reference the book's original story.

Messages can be created through a variety of methods and processes. These methods and processes can be instinctual and involve play and chance, methodical and involve steps that build upon one another, or visual, or they can incorporate writing as a conceptualization and development tool. Each approach can be used alone or in combination.

Design methodologies are largely qualitative but may include learning from measurable activities. Creation can be generative—that is, it can create new options as the process unfolds.

Creating Components

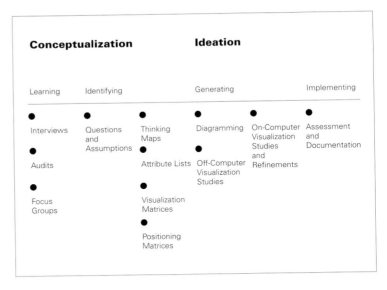

4.2
Creating components

Constraints
Constraints are the parameters
that bound a project. These can
include deadlines imposed
by the designer or client, laws
and ordinances, and cultural
conventions or norms.

The process of creating messages has two basic parts:
conceptualization and ideation. These parts may be put
together in linear or nonlinear order depending on a person's
creative process.

· Conceptualization

Concepts can be created through methods such as thinking
maps, attribute lists, and visual matrices.

· Ideation

Ideation refers to giving concepts visual form through pencil
sketches, image collages, and on-computer studies.

Creating Emotion

4.3
Identity symbol, 2010
EU Flag Design Competition Entry,
2010
Youngha Park

4.4
Identity symbol, 2010
EU Flag Design Competition Entry,
2010
Youngha Park

**"You've got to stand for
something. If customers know
what you stand for, they
build understanding. If they
understand they can begin to
connect. And if they can make
an emotional connection,
they build a preference."** [4]

Eric Scott, Creative Director
Wolff-Olins

Emotion is a powerful aspect of life and design. Although not
a process or method per se, it can be a strategic component.
Emotion is a way to connect with others.

Emotion can range from negative (fear) to positive (amusement),
simple (caring) to complex (patience), and primary (joy) to
secondary (optimism). Emotion is a reaction and can be based
on mood and gut feeling, as well as reasoned knowledge.

· Emotional Visuals

Emotion can be created through evocative imagery, expressive
typography, sensual materials, and simple visual juxtaposition.

· Emotional Connection

Emotional visuals create emotional connections. A design
strategy can form an emotional connection with a viewer to
elicit a specific response.

For a closer look, see Essay

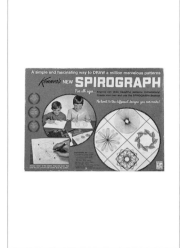

Play was used as a design
tool for the conceptualization of
a public playground.

4.5
Play as design tool
Ruedee Sarawutpaiboon

4.6
Spirograph

The Spirograph toy
shapes creativity
by limiting options.

Common Sense
Common-sense decisions and
opinions are based on experience,
intuition, and prior learning.

Play
In a design context, play refers
to spontaneous activities
used to create and evaluate forms
and messages. Playing with
Spirographs, Legos, and
Etch-a-Sketches, or otherwise
approaching a problem as
a game, may generate applicable
ideas not easily obtained through
methodical processes.

Intuition is knowledge or cognition without evident
rational thought and inference. Unique to each individual,
intuition is an extension of common sense, instinct,
and experience.

All methodologies and processes are guided by intuition.
While intuition alone is not a methodology, it is a
process and widely employed as the primary tool for
solving design problems.

4.7
Identity system, 2010
Client: Smartpad (Lenovo)
Jiuxue Zhang, design director
Lijian Wang, designer

4.8
Identity system study (above) and
application (right), 2010
Client: Smartpad (Lenovo)
Ning Zhang, strategist

This thoughtful identity is the result
of a step-by-step design process.

Concept
A concept is a thought, notion,
or idea upon which a project
is based and with which a
problem is solved.

Function
Function is a form's practical,
spiritual, cultural, or personal
purpose. An evaluation of
function includes asking why
the form was created, who
its audience is, how it will be
used, and what it will do.

In contrast to intuition-based approaches, methodical
approaches incorporate step-by-step procedures.
Problem solving tends to be methodical, particularly
for complex problems where large amounts of content are
involved or where a strategy involves many team members.
Research by definition is methodical and systematic.

A methodical approach doesn't rule out intuition, instinct,
play, or chance but rather serves as a guide to these
components. It allows designers to test all or selected
variables, thus ensuring that many possibilities can be
tested and the results reflected upon.

4.9
Writing in the design
process

Writing can be a useful and repeated component
of the design process, helping to clarify and articulate
ideas, record processes, and make assessments.

Writing
Writing offers a number of
advantages to the design process:

· Can be used as an aid to memory
and understanding
· May slow expression and thus
foster reflection
· Can allow ideas to be expressed
precisely, without any
extraneous information

Writing is a powerful aid in visual decision making. Words
that are visually arranged to express their meaning can help
visual learners (most graphic designers) conceptualize.
Visual learners tend to process information more easily as
shapes and patterns.

Visually arranged writing can be a simple list of words that
shows relationships. It initiates the cognitive process of
giving physical form to an idea and helps us form images
in our minds.

Questions

· What are the important graphic design methodologies and processes?

· How do they originate, and how are they applied?

Assumptions

· The study of methodologies is largely ignored in graphic design education.

· A visually concise approach can make a contribution to design education.

For a closer look, see Exercises

4.10
Question and assumptions used to develop this book

4.11
Listing and prioritizing questions and assumptions

This collaborative workshop explored methods and processes for generating, prioritizing, and valuing questions and assumptions on chosen subjects.

Questions
There are three basic types of research questions.

· Descriptive questions seek to characterize the qualities and traits of something.
· Relational questions look at the connections among variables.
· Causal questions attempt to determine whether one variable influences another.

Consciously or subconsciously, every design you create is based on the questions the project is intended to answer and on assumptions about the audience. Writing down the questions and assumptions may begin a project's targeting phase.

· Questions

A question can address a project's value, the type of response to expect, the target audience, and how success will be determined. It can be answered with a simple yes or no, or require a lengthier response.

· Assumptions

Assumptions are beliefs that something is true and are the foundation of all research. Assumptions may include audience familiarity with a visual language or digital interaction method. Assumptions can be formed through interviews, market research, previous work, or experience.

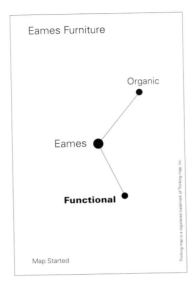

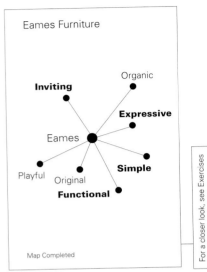

4.12
Thinking
map
started

A word that identifies
the project's primary
characteristic is placed
in the center.

4.13
Thinking map
completed

As words related to
the center word
are added, the map
radiates outward.

John Bowers Introduction to Graphic Design Methodologies and Processes

For a closer look, see Exercises

Brainstorming
Formalized by Alex F. Osburn
in the early 1950s,
brainstorming is the fast,
criticism-free generation
of ideas.

A thinking map is an effective method for generating
concepts. Together with an attribute list, it can help you
create and classify ideas and develop focus.

· Thinking Maps

A thinking map is a diagram that begins with a single word.
From that word, related descriptive words are chosen
by free association. The related words are placed intuitively
in an expanding fashion to further understanding of the
center word.

· Attribute Lists

An attribute list is a collection of adjectives that can help
define the personality of a project and can be used to drive
visual decision making, including font choices, color palettes,
and the like. An example attribute list for this page could
be: accessible, straightforward, clear, concise, and structured.

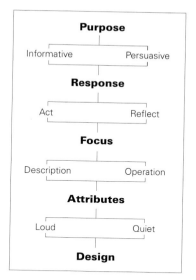

Purpose

Informative   Persuasive

Response

Act   Reflect

Focus

Description   Operation

Attributes

Loud   Quiet

Design

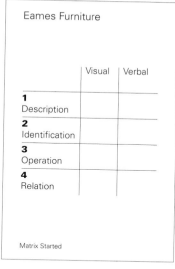

Eames Furniture

	Visual	Verbal
1 Description		
2 Identification		
3 Operation		
4 Relation		

Matrix Started

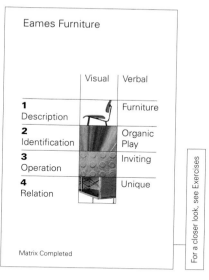

Eames Furniture

	Visual	Verbal
1 Description		Furniture
2 Identification		Organic Play
3 Operation		Inviting
4 Relation		Unique

Matrix Completed

For a closer look, see Exercises

4.14 Decision tree — Moving from top to bottom, "either-or" options are presented.

4.15 Visual matrix — While a decision tree helps clarify a message's purpose, desired response, and visual attributes, a visual matrix focuses on specific aspects of the message.

Decision Tree
A decision tree is a visual pathway that provides "either-or" and "if-then" options.

Visual Matrix
A visual matrix is a series of quadrants in which images (literal, abstract, or symbolic) and words are placed that describe aspects of a theme, subject, or object.

Decision trees and visual matrices provide another method for approaching problems and generating ideas.

· Decision Tree

A decision tree presents options for each stage of the design process. It is often part of the visual identity guidelines that help focus an entity's messages.

· Visual Matrix

A visual matrix helps expand thinking through its links between the components. Matrix components may include the description (what is it?), identification (what defines it?), operation (how does it work?), and relation (how is it situated?).

Alphabetical (A-Z)

· Central America
· North America
· South America

Continuum (Size)

· South America
· North America
· Central America

Location (North to South)

· North America
· Central America
· South America

4.16
Listing types

Presentations
and listing types
can imply
value judgments.

4.17
Depiction of the Western hemisphere.

Information
Information architect Richard
Saul Wurman identifies five
ways in which information can
be organized:

· Alphabetically (A through Z)
· Category (based on an
object's type)
· Continuum (relative sizes,
distances, heights, and value
[good to bad])
· Location (physical place)
· Time (time or date of an event
or action)

Prioritizing content is necessary to make information
accessible and meaningful. The prioritizing process involves
listing content, grouping content, editing content, and
labeling content. Commonly asked questions include:

· What is an engaging way to present content?
· What value is suggested by the presentation method?
· Does the presentation method match the viewer's visual
decoding abilities?

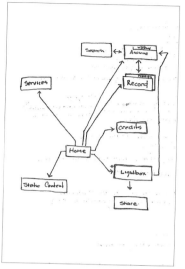

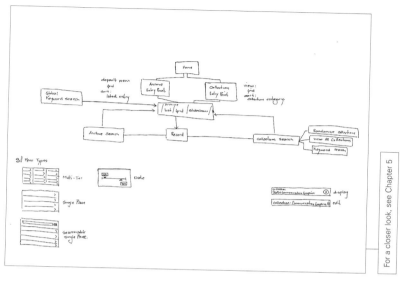

4.18
Organizational sketches for
Design Archives Website, 2010
Client: AIGA
Second Story Interactive Studios

4.19
Organizational sketches for
Design Archives Website, 2010
Client: AIGA
Second Story Interactive Studios

Diagramming is a method of planning, explaining, and giving form to ideas. It can be used to record an event, describe a process, or relate a body of information.

Once learned, the symbols employed in diagramming can concisely explain and convey ideas that would be difficult to clarify through other types of visual representation or written form.

For a closer look, see Chapter 5

4.20
Sketches (left) and final identity
symbol (right), 2006
Client: Obama presidential campaign
Sender LLC

Multiple hand-drawn directions led to
a final symbol.

Directions
In the context of graphic
design, directions can indicate
multiple ways of visually
solving a problem.

Iteration
An iteration is the repetition of
a sequence of operations.

Generative Work
Generative work builds upon
itself, creating new ideas and
outcomes in the process.

Determining content, developing a concept, and giving
form to the concept involve conceptualization and ideation.

During the conceptualization phase of a project, ideas are
often developed through hand-drawn sketches. The ideation
phase includes creating multiple directions and options
that reinforce earlier design decisions or help lead a client
to a particular choice. The process may differ depending on
the designer and the project.

Creating Emphasizing

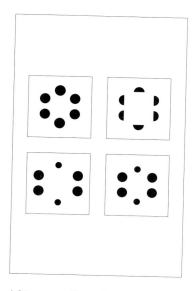

4.21
Gestalt
principles

Top to bottom and left
to right: closure,
continuance, proximity,
and similarity.

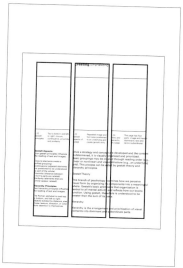

4.22
Gestalt
aspects of
a page

Repeated image and
font sizes positioned
to an underlying grid
create gestalt unity.

4.23
Parts and
hierarchy of
a page

This page has four
parts: image and header
(dominant), text and
terms (subordinate).

Gestalt Aspects
Four gestalt principles influence
the reading of text and images:

· Closure (elements create a
unified grouping)
· Continuance (adjacent elements
are positioned to be understood
as part of the whole)
· Proximity (distance's between
a form's parts are related)
· Similarity (elements that are
similar appear related)

Hierarchy Principles
Two hierarchy principles influence
the reading of text and images:

· The Roman alphabet is read top
to bottom, and left to right.
· Objects isolated by distance, size,
shape, texture, direction, or color
draw attention to themselves.

Once a strategy and concept are developed and the content
is determined, it is visually organized and prioritized.
Basic groupings may be created through reading order (e.g.,
linear or nonlinear) and visual structure (e.g., an underlying
grid). This process can be aided by gestalt theory and
hierarchy principles.

· Gestalt Theory

This branch of psychology examines how we perceive
visual form by organizing its components into a meaningful
whole. Gestalt's basic premise is that organization is
central to all mental activity and reflects how our brains
function. Using gestalt, the whole is understood to be
greater than the sum of its parts.

· Hierarchy

Hierarchy is the arrangement and prioritization of visual
elements into dominant and subordinate parts.

59

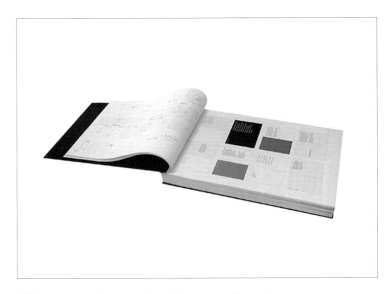

4.24
Process book

A process book documents the design process
and helps explain decision making.

Process Book
A process book is the
documentation of a project's
design process. It typically
includes edited examples
of research, inspiration,
conceptualization, and ideation.
It is helpful in assessing and
presenting a project.

Documenting a completed project is important in
determining its success. Creating documentation
by recording, saving, editing, and organizing verbal and
visual processes and materials used in a project aids in
project assessment because it explains decision making.

A project's documentation can also be useful for
developing future projects, furthering the quality and
consistency of working processes.

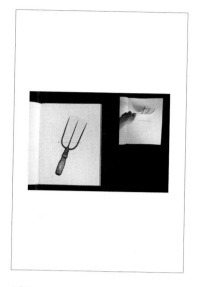

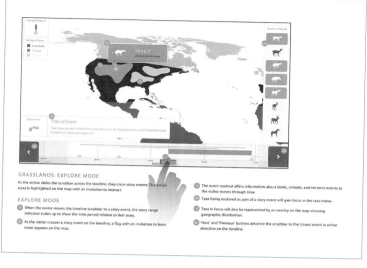

GRASSLANDS: EXPLORE MODE

As the visitor slides the scrubber across the timeline, they cross story events. The active story is highlighted on the map with an invitation to interact.

EXPLORE MODE

01 When the visitor moves the timeline scrubber to a story event, the story range indicator scales up to show the time period relative to that story.

02 As the visitor crosses a story event on the timeline, a flag with an invitation to learn more appears on the map.

03 The event readout offers information about biotic, climatic, and tectonic events as the visitor moves through time.

04 Taxa being explored as part of a story event will gain focus in the taxa menu.

05 Taxa in focus will also be represented by an overlay on the map showing geographic distribution.

06 'Next' and 'Previous' buttons advance the scrubber to the closest event in either direction on the timeline.

4.25
Billy Rabbit:
An American Adaptation, 2006
Ann Tyler

4.26
Wireframe for Grasslands Kiosk, 2009
Client: Natural History Museum of
Los Angeles County
Second Story Interactive Studios

Tyler tells a story of oppression by encouraging physical engagement. Second Story tells a story of evolution by providing the user with multiple access points and choices.

Storytelling
Storytelling is the act of relating and sharing ideas from a given point of view. Stories traditionally have a beginning, middle, and end through which elements or characters are introduced and interact as the plot unfolds. Storytelling is a timeless activity evolved from early cultural rituals used to inform, persuade, explain, and entertain.

In graphic design, storytelling is expressed by sharing a work's concept with a client and through the work itself.

· Presentation Storytelling

Verbally presenting a work as a story can personalize abstract ideas and provide a context that allows others to better grasp its concept.

· Design as Storytelling

A work's story may be told through words as well as images. Interactive media allow users to more fully shape a story's reading, resulting in nonlinear experiences based on user participation.

John Bowers Introduction to Graphic Design Methodologies and Processes

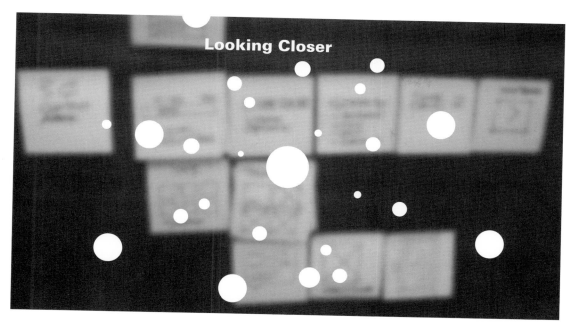

Looking Closer

Concepts

Interpreting
Rick Valicenti (Thirst Studio)
Antonio Alcalá (Studio A)

Targeting
Julie Beeler and Brad Johnson
(Second Story Interactive Studios)

Creating
Michelle Bowers
Sol Sender (Sender LLC)

This chapter examines a select group of individuals and their collaborations, which employ a range of methodologies in solving diverse design problems.

Looking Closer

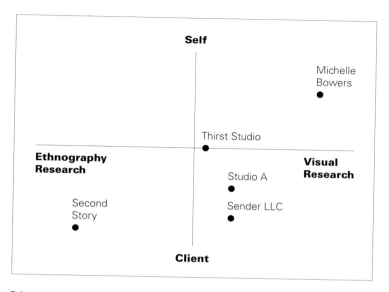

5.1
Positioning of select individual and collaborative work

This chapter explores a single project or related body of work from five select designers and studios introduced earlier.

The diversity of approaches to contemporary design problems is exemplified in Rick Valicenti's application of learning gained from self-generated experiments to client-associated work, Antonio Alcalá's use of discussion and expansive idea generation, Julie Beeler's and Brad Johnson's integration of audience feedback and collaborative problem solving, Michelle Bowers' reliance on intuition and experience, and Sol Sender's use of generative processes and market analysis.

While the designers differ in how they create forms, use visual languages, and involve their audiences, they are remarkably similar in their reliance on methods and processes unique to their needs and interests.

5.2
Page spreads from
Intelligent Design: Creating an Evolved Red vs. Blue State of Mind, 2005
Client and Design: Thirst Studio

This self-published tabloid explores intersecting issues of consumerism and religion expressed through a computer program.

Rick Valicenti

Rick Valicenti is the founder and principal of Thirst Studio, located in Chicago, Illinois. His work is included in the permanent collection of the Cooper-Hewitt National Design Museum, and has been published in *Graphis*, *CA*, and *ID*, among many others. He has been awarded the President's Design Award from The National Endowment for the Arts, and is an AIGA medalist. He holds an MFA in photography from the University of Iowa.

Thirst Studio uses self-generated projects as a way of informing client-associated projects. The Intelligent Design and Third Coast Audio projects are related in that both use computer programs to generate form.

· Intelligent Design

Programming in this project is used to translate each word of the Book of Genesis into a Coke or Pepsi can.

· Third Coast Audio

This project used programming and sound to make audio visual. Like snowflakes and thumbprints, voiceprints and the designs based on voiceprints are unique.

Intelligent Design Project Objective

· To create a visual narrative using commonly consumed objects as social commentary.

Processes

· Establish Point of View
· Choose Objects and Text
· Develop Concept
· Write Computer Program
· Create Design Mockups
· Finalize Page Designs

5.3
Project objective and processes

5.4
Page spreads from
Intelligent Design: Creating an Evolved Red vs. Blue State of Mind, 2005
Client and Design: Thirst Studio

Pop cans replacing the text of the Book of Genesis serve as social commentary.

Intelligent Design: Creating an Evolved Red vs. Blue State of Mind Team Members
· Rick Valicenti, Design Director
· Gina Garza and John Pobojewski, Designers
· Robb Irrgang, Programmer
· Gina Garza, Photographer

Third Coast Audio Team Members
· Rick Valicenti, Design Director
· John Pobojewski and Bud Rodecker, Designers
· Thea Dickman, Photographer

· Learning and Identifying

An early step in the Intelligent Design project was the creation of a computer program that would replace each word in the Book of Genesis with a pop can.

Similarly, early in the Third Coast Audio project, a computer program was created that would record the unique voiceprint of each company associate, with external contours controlled by volume and color controlled by the speaker's pitch.

· Generating and Implementing

The patterns generated by the Intelligent Design computer program were set into oversized pages to heighten their presence. The voiceprints generated by the Third Coast Audio program were placed onto business cards (each containing the cardholder's audio expression of his or her name) and posters (each superimposing an associate's contour with a visualization of that person's audio expression).

67

Third Coast Audio Project Objective

· To create an identity system that uses sound to customize each expression.

Processes

· Develop Concept
· Plan Computerized Sound Expressions
· Create Design Mockups
· Finalize Designs

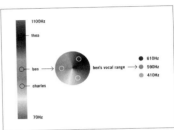

5.5
Project objective and processes

5.6
Sound visualization study (top) and process diagram (below), 2009
Client: Third Coast Audio
Thirst Studio

Q+A with Rick Valicenti

How did Intelligent Design influence the Third Coast Audio project?

"Intelligent Design was a seminal project on many levels and its valuable impact continues to be present. While we were able to layer our cultural commentary on the religious right and America's political conflict between the red and blue states, it is the discovery of automating content within the production process that has liberated our creative process. Not only are we able to streamline the production process, we now can conceive solutions in ways we had never been able to before." [5]

How does your photography background shape your current work?

"Having received my MFA in photography, I do tend to see the world through the image. It is through this lens that I also see the manipulative powers available to a designed image. I like to think I am able to direct an image-centric message with a slightly different sense of how it will resonate and communicate once it has entered the real world." [6]

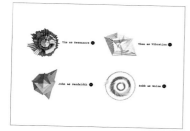

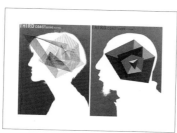

5.7
Sound visualization (top) and
application (bottom), 2009
Client: Third Coast Audio
Thirst Studio

5.8
Cards (top) and posters (bottom)
proposal, 2009
Client: Third Coast Audio
Thirst Studio

5.9
Poster application proposal, 2009
Client: Third Coast Audio
Thirst Studio

Q+A with Rick Valicenti

**How does your self-generated
work relate to your client-
associated work?**

"For many years, I have advocated
a model of practice where play
and discovery are fundamental
to a healthy and sustainable design
process and output. It is through
an investment of real time to
pursue the interests within the
studio that our collective
sensibilities are awakened and our
ability to attract more interesting
opportunities is alive.

"When professional opportunities
come to us, we do not have
to look for a fresh stream of
consciousness because we are
already surrounded by many. It is
at this moment when we invite the
client assignment into our world

and at the same time we share with
our client our cultural interests,
our technological curiosities, and
our design sensibilities.

"I often ask what a design studio
experience would be like without
self-generated work and all I can
see is a studio cluttered with books
and annuals marked with Post-its.
This is not the only place where
new ideas gestate." [7]

5.10
Page from *To Sleep, Perchance to Dream*, 2008
Client: Folger Shakespeare Library
Studio A

Antonio Alcalá
Antonio Alcalá is the principal of Studio A, a graphic design studio in Alexandria, Virginia. Studio A has received critical praise from numerous publications and organizations. Antonio is an American Institute of Graphic Arts, Washington, D.C., Fellow Medalist. He is also a professor at the Corcoran College of Art + Design in Washington, D.C., and provides guidance on the design of all U.S. postage stamps as an appointed member of the Postmaster General's Citizen's Stamp Advisory Committee.

Antonio Alcalá's approach to solving design problems is based on text analysis and visual comparisons. In his studio, he relies on a team of designers to generate, evaluate, and develop concepts. Working with repeat clients, some for over 10 years, he builds and uses relationships that inform his design process.

His process is largely linear and moves from rough ideas to refined forms. His emphasis on thoughtful typography integrated with simple physical forms is influenced by his study under three important figures of contemporary graphic design: Paul Rand, Bradbury Thompson, and Armin Hofmann. Much of his work has been done for museums in Washington, D.C., and reflects his interest in history, cultivated through his undergraduate history degree studies at Yale University.

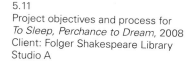

Project Objectives

· To create a catalog for an exhibition on sleep that reflects Renaissance writing styles and expresses the mysteries of sleep.

Process

· Analyze Text
· Create Sketches
· Study Imagery and Typography
· Define Format and Structure
· Design Pages
· Oversee Printing

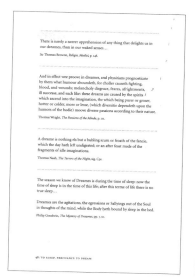

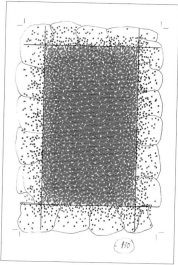

5.11
Project objectives and process for
To Sleep, Perchance to Dream, 2008
Client: Folger Shakespeare Library
Studio A

5.12
Page from
To Sleep, Perchance to Dream, 2008
Client: Folger Shakespeare Library
Studio A

5.13
Pencil sketches for
To Sleep, Perchance to Dream, 2008
Client: Folger Shakespeare Library
Studio A

Folger Shakespeare Library in Washington, D.C., houses the world's largest collection of Shakespeare materials and other rare Renaissance books

· Learning and Identifying

To Sleep, Perchance to Dream is composed of seven sections, such as "Sleep Metaphors," each with excerpts about sleep and dreams written in England during the Renaissance. The concept was to create a visual analogy to dreams. As Antonio describes it, often in dreams two or more incongruent items appear, yet the narrative holds together.

· Generating and Implementing

After Antonio and his team of designers had read and discussed the text multiple times, sections were identified that could be highlighted typographically. Sketches and digital studies followed that determined page proportions and size, grid structure, and font choices and usage. A pattern of overlapping lines was designed for each section opener. As the book progressed, the pattern became more diffused, alluding to the experience of drifting off to sleep and entering the dream state.

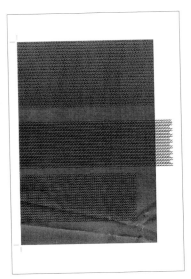

5.14
Study for
To Sleep, Perchance to Dream, 2008
Client: Folger Shakespeare Library
Studio A

5.15
Page from
To Sleep, Perchance to Dream, 2008
Client: Folger Shakespeare Library
Studio A

Q+A with Antonio Alcalá

Describe your working process

"My process tends to be linear but occasionally unpredictable. With most of our catalogues for the Folger, the process begins with a visit to the Library to meet the curator and look at examples of the materials to be included. We also discuss what important ideas need to be conveyed to the reader. Afterwards, I'll read the manuscript, look at the images to be included, and take notes.

"At that point, I usually start to sketch ideas on 8.5 x 11 white copier paper. I'll review these with one or more designers in the office. We have no set protocol…

just sitting around a conference table, talking and sketching some more. I'll then turn an 'approved' direction into a mockup to circulate in the office. When that looks good, it's presented to the client for review. We provide only one direction. Generally, this is approved with minor alterations. We then move forward with the book layout."[8]

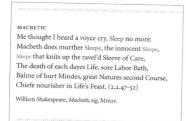

MACBETH:

Me thought I heard a voyce cry, Sleep no more:
Macbeth does murther Sleepe, the innocent Sleepe,
Sleepe that knits up the ravel'd Sleeve of Care,
The death of each dayes Life, sore Labor Bath,
Balme of hurt Mindes, great Natures second Course,
Chiefe nourisher in Life's Feast. (2.2.47–52)

William Shakespeare, *Macbeth*, sig. Mm2v.

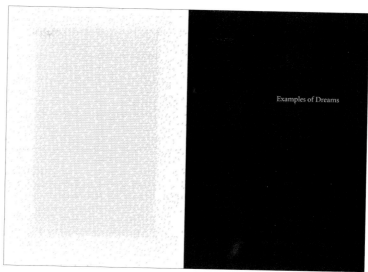

Examples of Dreams

5.16
Detail and double-page spread from
To Sleep, Perchance to Dream, 2008
Client: Folger Shakespeare Library
Antonio Alcalá, Studio A

5.17
Double-page spread from
To Sleep, Perchance to Dream, 2008
Client: Folger Shakespeare Library
Antonio Alcalá, Studio A

Q+A with Antonio Alcalá

Do you write or edit content?

"I do, on rare occasions, write copy, but never on book projects. I might tell our client how they might edit their content to better communicate their ideas/message. When it does happen, I think it makes the designer/client relationship stronger. The client recognizes we are not just concerned with the visual, but also with content."[9]

How important is storytelling?

"This is a crucial part of our practice. As a designer, I am interested in how I can help reveal content through the design. Sometimes the attempt may be quite overt, but often it is a subtle part of the design. Revealing the thought process behind design decisions and the choices that enhance the content help make the client feel more secure and confident in the design.

"With books, the designer is often working with content that the author/curator has been working with for many, many years. They appreciate a designer who treats their work respectfully and clearly explains decisions behind the design."[10]

John Bowers Introduction to Graphic Design Methodologies and Processes

5.18
Home page of
Design Archives Website, 2010
Client: AIGA
Second Story Interactive Studios

**Julie Beeler and
Brad Johnson**
Julie Beeler and Brad Johnson
are principals of Second Story
Interactive Studios, an
interactive media design studio
in Portland, Oregon. Second
Story focuses on narrative
storytelling and interactive
installations for museums,
including the Smithsonian
Museum, Washington, D.C., and
the Library of Congress.
They have earned awards from
ID, *Communication Arts*, and
American Institute of Graphic
Arts, among many others.

Second Story's name is based on the belief that there are
two stories in interactive media (such as a website). The first
story is presented by the website's content before the user
interacts with it. The second story is created when a user
interacts with the content and shapes a story—an individual
path of retrieving, reading, and responding to content.

In interactive form, users are provided with a variety of
navigation options. Often, each option can uniquely shape
the reading and understanding of content. Effective design
anticipates how those paths will create a story through
the users' choices.

Project Objectives

· To create a design archive website that empowers users by allowing for the editing and comparing of content, and a variety of retrieval options.

Process

· Analyze Function/Content
· Write Project Brief
· Create Wireframes and Look and Feel
· Conduct Navigation Studies
· Design Site Architecture
· Design, Program, and Test

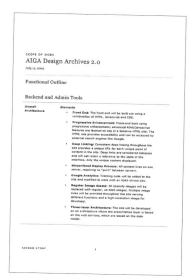

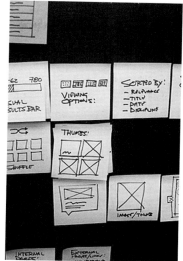

5.19
Project objectives and process for Design Archives Website, 2010
Client: AIGA
Second Story Interactive Studios

5.20
Project brief for
Design Archives Website, 2010
Client: AIGA
Second Story Interactive Studios

5.21
Conceptualization process for
Design Archives Website, 2010
Client: AIGA
Second Story Interactive Studios

**AIGA Design Archives
Website Team Members
Second Story
Interactive Studios**
· Julie Beeler, Executive Director
· Brad Johnson, Creative Director
· Shoam Thomas, Lead Interaction Designer
· Kieran Lynn, Designer
· Thomas Wester, Technology Director
· David Brewer, Lead Systems Developer
· Donald Richardson, Developer
· Michael Neault, Production Coordinator
· Kate Wolf, Quality Assurance
AIGA
· Denise Wood, Chief Operations Officer
· Heather Strelecki, Information Specialist
· Gabriela Mirensky, Competitions and Exhibitions Director
· Lydia Mann, Web Director

· Learning and Identifying

The studio's 25 members include strategists, consultants, planners, concept developers, programmers, copywriters, and designers. These members are divided into three groups: design, technology, and production. Group members are assigned to projects and work together to create an end result and its story.

The Design Archives Website project began with a series of meetings to discuss the website's purpose and function. The studio then wrote a project brief that detailed the required work and deadlines. Upon approval by the client, focus group meetings were held that further clarified the website's role and design possibilities.

Conceptualization processes, including one using Post-it notes, were used to identify and organize content and user access to content. This allowed the team to see and relocate groups of content and navigational functions.

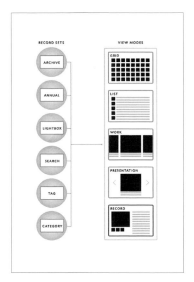

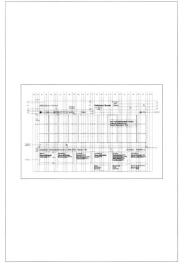

5.22
Information architecture diagrams for
Design Archives Website, 2010
Client: AIGA
Second Story Interactive Studios

5.23
Information architecture study for
Design Archives Website, 2010
Client: AIGA
Second Story Interactive Studios

· Generating and Implementing

Concepts generated in the earlier steps were refined and
made visual. This included diagrams of the website's
functions. The design team studied website content on
various pages, the visual organization of pages, and font
and color usage.

They then conducted navigation studies that explored
how interactive elements, including buttons, could
be designed. In the final phase, a beta (prototype) site was
posted and tested by users to gain initial feedback before
the website was finalized.

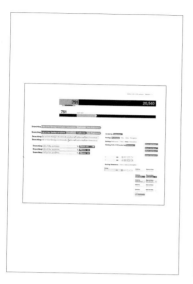

5.24
Component study for
Design Archives Website, 2010
Client: AIGA
Second Story Interactive Studios

5.25
Information architecture (wireframe) study for
Design Archives Website, 2010
Client: AIGA
Second Story Interactive Studios

Q+A with Julie Beeler and Brad Johnson

How do you learn about your target audience?

"We initially hosted a focus group with educators, students, designers, and AIGA chapter members. Invitees were asked about their experience with the current version of the Design Archives Website, and subsequently presented with wireframes to review. To generate further discussion, we asked a specific set of questions about the interaction design and the various user features and components. The feedback from these discussions had a large influence on how we prioritized features for this project." [11]

What verbal or written processes do you use?

"The project kicked off with a lively and constructive brainstorming session. Each team member brought ideas written on post-it notes, along with drawings, diagrams, and inspirational clippings. All of the ideas were then assembled on a board to generate and guide the discussion. During the meeting, the drawings took shape into more coherent ideas, and patterns emerged.

After the brainstorming sessions, content strategists, interaction designers, and the creative director took the jumble of ideas and proceeded to categorize, condense, combine, and refine them into treatments and concept packages." [12]

5.26
Selection feature (image) for
Design Archives Website, 2010
Client: AIGA
Second Story Interactive Studios

Q+A with Julie Beeler and Brad Johnson

To what extent do you employ quantitative research?

"For this project, we conducted two rounds of usability testing on a working beta site. For the first study, we took the beta to a design-oriented community gathering and let people explore the site. We didn't apply any formal strategy for testing; we wanted to observe how people experienced the site with little or no guidance.

"The second round was more focused. We invited a group of graphic design students from Portland State University to do usability testing. Students spent a total of 10 minutes with the site. The first five minutes were dedicated to freeform exploration, and the second five minutes were dedicated to guided prompts." [13]

How important is storytelling in your practice?

"Storytelling and narrative is at the very heart of every project done at the studio. You can often overhear team members assessing projects by asking, 'What is the story we're trying to tell?'

"However, storytelling in interactive media offers challenges and opportunities that differ from those in traditional linear storytelling. The evolution of interactive media means the story no longer flows in one direction, from the one to the many. Through a framework of possibilities that visitors use to weave their stories, the narrative is only visible in hindsight—when their paths are revealed." [14]

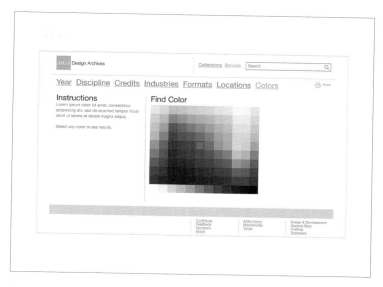

5.27
Selection feature (color) for
Design Archives Website, 2010
Client: AIGA
Second Story Interactive Studios

**Q+A with Julie Beeler and
Brad Johnson**

**Describe your working
process.**

"Second Story has an internal
process that guides our overall
development of interactive media
experiences. This process can be
visualized as a musical scale,
with components like notes on
the scale and concurrent phases
layered like chords. The document
is called the 'process score,' and
it's a particularly germane visual
metaphor because many of the
principles of music can be applied
to process.

"Some projects demand a rigid,
Western-style interpretation
of studio process, while others
demand a more modal,
improvisational approach. In either
case, you have to be flexible
and respond to the needs of each
project. If process becomes too
robotic, you risk losing sight of the
big picture.

"The score for most projects
roughly follows these phases:
concept development, user
experience, design development,
user testing, production, and
quality assurance. Each phase
involves deliveries, feedback, and
discussions with the client and
key partners.

To continue with the music
metaphor, the team for each
project is like a jazz session, and
the interpretation of the score
varies according to the talents of
the players." [15]

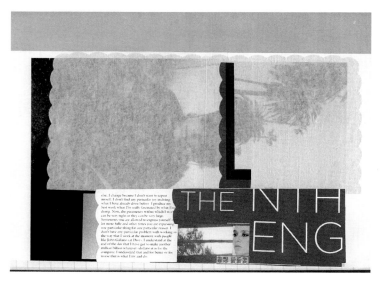

5.28
Page spread from *Carbon Gluebook*, 2007
Found printed material and self-photographed imagery glued in found book
Michelle Bowers

Michelle Bowers
Michelle Bowers is an assistant professor at the University of Massachusetts, Dartmouth. Her work has been published by the American Institute of Graphic Arts, the *Type Directors Club*, and *Graphic Design: The New Basics*.

Michelle Bowers uses juxtaposed print imagery glued into discarded library books to create visually rich narratives. The subject matter and typographic design of these found books are the departure point for her self-generated design work. They are also an inspiration for her applied design work, such as posters and catalogs.

Gluebooks contain little readable text, and the book titles are matter-of-fact, referencing either the place a book was done or its dominant color, e.g., *Yellow Gluebook*. Reading order and interpretation are not explicitly directed, but instead guided through the use of cropped letters and images. The viewer is asked to put the pieces together to create a narrative and to derive meaning, an experience that departs from that provided by many mass-produced books meant to be read from beginning to end and offering a single interpretation.

Project Objectives

· To create visual narratives using found printed material and discarded books.

Process

· Find and Choose Book
· Find and Choose Imagery
· Develop Concept
· Create Design Mockups
· Finalize Page Designs
· Glue Parts in Book

5.29
Project objectives and process for gluebooks
Michelle Bowers

5.30
Collage parts for gluebooks
Found printed material and self-photographed imagery
Michelle Bowers

5.31
Collage parts for gluebooks
Found printed material and self-photographed imagery
Michelle Bowers

· Learning and Identifying

A gluebook project begins with finding and analyzing discarded library books, followed by sorting through collections of popular culture fashion magazines. Provocative imagery that can be used with minimal cropping—or mundane imagery that becomes provocative through juxtaposition—is combined with cropped letters and lines of type.

· Generating and Implementing

Michelle's process of placing image and type together is largely intuitive, honed by experience and directed by the message of the original imagery and text of the found book. Dynamic visual rhythms are created from page to page as dominant colors, patterns, and focal points change. The book's consistent page size maintains congruence among the many different page collages.

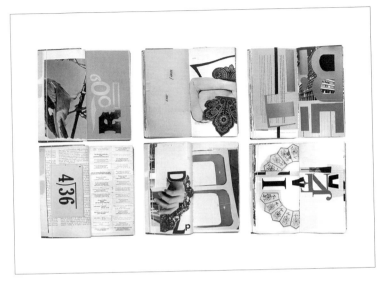

5.32
Page spreads from *Cranbrook Gluebook*, 2003
Found printed material and self-photographed imagery glued in found book
Michelle Bowers

Q+A with Michelle Bowers

Describe your working process.

"I sift and sort through formal and contextual interests, trying out this and that, seeing what bubbles up. My work emerges through reinterpretation and hybridization. I search for connections and the resonance between things.

"This investigation demonstrates my connection to the world, to understanding my own attractions and desires. It also serves as the background for my professional work, and even ends up foregrounded through display and publication. Obviously not all designers work this way; many make the client relationship the starting place for problem solving and ideas." [16]

What verbal or written processes do you use?

"I often explore a writing process developed by the Dada artist and experimental poet Tristan Tzara. In following Tzara's prescription, poetry is created by cutting up appropriated text and rearranging it in random order. The recontextualization creates new meaning; associations occur both accidentally and rationally. This use of found content and chance placement has done much to inform both my ideation process and formal aesthetic." [17]

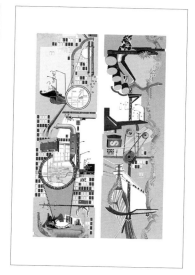

5.33
Art Department posters, 2008
Printed offset
Client: Kendall College of Art and
Design, Michelle Bowers

5.34
University Viewbook, 2003
Printed offset
Client: Grand Valley State University
Michelle Bowers

5.35
Viewbook interpretative maps, 2003
Printed offset
Client: Grand Valley State University
Michelle Bowers

Q+A with Michelle Bowers

How does the book form shape your process?

"I use discarded library books as the format for my visual studies. Because these books present a specific history and intention, I find myself not only applying to their pages the themes and images I am interested in, but also reacting to their already-ordered nature. I work between the lines and in the margins of another individual's published work, collaborating and conspiring with the original content to create a new, redefined interpretation.

"These books are an integral part of my design process. They have become a way to create form and content. I often write poetry, indexes/lists, and notes from research and reading." [18]

Do you primarily work alone?

"I usually work alone, however I often invite artists, writers, and designers to join me in my studio. For me it is important to be part of a creative community. The interaction and sharing of ideas, no matter how remote or seemingly unrelated, is inspirational and impacts my work and thinking." [19]

5.36
Studies for Identity symbol, 2006
Client: Obama presidential campaign
Sender LLC

Replacing the letter O with an image
allowed for the visualization of a broader
set of ideas and the ability to evoke
more emotion.

Sol Sender
Sol Sender is an associate partner
with VSA Partners, a design
firm in Chicago, Illinois, and is
principal of the Sender LLC
design firm. His work has been
published in *The New York Times*,
Communication Arts, and *How*
magazine, among others.
He has been a speaker at
numerous conferences, including
the AIGA, the American Center
for Design, the Art Directors Club,
and ICOGRADA World
Design Congress.

**Obama Presidential
Campaign Symbol Team
Sender LLC**
· Sol Sender, Creative Director
· Amanda Gentry and Andy Keene,
Designers

The Barack Obama presidential campaign was sparked by
its identity symbol. The image of the sun rising over the
horizon evokes a sense of hope, echoing the idea of Obama
as a symbol of progress and change to his supporters.

In 2006, Sol Sender was approached about designing a
symbol for the campaign. He had never designed a political
identity but took on the project with the goal of creating
a symbol for the campaign as much as for the candidate
himself. The result was immediately memorable.

Project Objective

· To create a symbol
for then-candidate
Barack Obama's
presidential campaign

Processes

· Meet with Campaign Team
· Make First-Round Version
· Present First-Round
· Make Second-Round Version
· Present Second-Round
· Finalize Chosen Symbol

5.37
Project objective and processes

5.38
First-round identity symbol
versions, 2006
Client: Obama presidential campaign
Sender LLC

5.39
First-round identity symbol
versions, 2006
Client: Obama presidential campaign
Sender LLC

· Learning and Identifying

The entire design process took less than two weeks and
consisted of two rounds of exploration presentations.
The first round of designs included eight options that varied
both typographically and conceptually, yet were inspired
by then-candidate Obama's campaign theme of hope
and change.

· Generating and Implementing

The second round of designs quickly generated a final
outcome. Once the letter O shape was chosen, studies were
conducted to refine it. Presentations were made to Obama's
chief strategist, from which Obama gave his opinion.

5.40
Second-round identity symbol
version, 2006
Client: Obama presidential campaign
Sender LLC

5.41
Second-round identity symbol
version, 2006
Client: Obama presidential campaign
Sender LLC

Q+A with Sol Sender

**What were the unique
challenges of this project?**

"We had only two weeks to develop
the identity. Generally, it takes
us four to six weeks to develop
three to four options for
presentation. There was obviously
a lot of excitement and passion
about the project, though, so we
were able to develop eight to nine
options within about a week's
time. In this case, excitement and
passion were closely tied to a deep
understanding of the significance
of the candidacy and message.
As a result, there was little need
for multiple discussions about
differentiation and positioning—
aspects of brand identity projects
that can, in other instances, take a
number of weeks or even months.

"We were also charged with doing
'something new'—an ambiguous
requirement, to be sure, but
one that we also immediately
understood. As we surveyed
the history of American
presidential campaign graphics,
we saw little creativity or
innovation. The bar was ready
to be raised." [20]

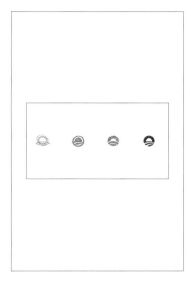

5.42
Identity symbol sketch, 2006
Client: Obama presidential campaign
Sender LLC

5.43
Final identity symbol, 2006
Client: Obama presidential campaign
Sender LLC

Q+A with Sol Sender

How did the symbol's message evolve once implemented?

"Once the identity was developed, managing its usage was challenging. We did develop guidelines, but it was difficult to ensure their distribution. It was only when the campaign brought in a full-time staff of designers that the execution became consistent—and consistently excellent. It should be noted, though, that the grassroots use of the logo was encouraged. These instances were naturally inconsistent, but beautifully so. They did not emanate directly from the campaign, so variations in quality were not a reflection on the quality of the candidate. Instead, they communicated a diverse and powerful support for him." [21]

How has this project changed your thoughts on design?

"It was actually this grassroots use of the logo that most impacted my thinking about design. I had never seen a logo take on so many forms and undergo so many adaptations. I notice this more now, even with brands like IBM and AT&T. Brand expression, as a practice, is evolving. Consumers are more savvy and skeptical. They value authenticity, transparency, and variety. As a result, our passion for design may have more currency in the future. When modernism arrived in the United States, pure design and commerce interacted more seamlessly. Since then, we've gone through decades of marketing devoid of design intelligence. It just wasn't valued. I think that might be changing." [22]

John Bowers Introduction to Graphic Design Methodologies and Processes

Timeline

The following timeline provides an overview of the primary methodologies and processes of graphic design over the past 100 years. It shows these in relation to cultural and societal changes, and through select resulting designs.

Earlier in the past century, there was a distinct and linear progression from one movement to another, but at present the movements tend to overlap; both convergence and divergence are occurring at the same time as a result of technological and societal changes. While technology is converging (e.g., cell phones can send, receive, transact, record, and archive), audiences are fragmenting, in part as a result of the Internet. Contemporary methodologies and processes are either leading or responding to these changes.

While design methodologies and processes are largely rooted in the Bauhaus and Ulm schools of design, they have moved beyond simple problem solving to complex forms, including those based on ethnographic research. Most recently, the study of methodologies has been advanced with the introduction of several doctorate programs in design research. As discussed earlier in the book and as presented in the timeline, many graphic design methodologies are derived from other disciplines, including industrial design.

Bauhaus
Bauhaus (1919—1933) was a highly influential German design school that led the modernist movement by integrating fine and applied arts.

Ulm
The Ulm School of Design (1953—1968) was a German design school that systematically integrated science and art into a problem-solving design curriculum.

John Bowers Introduction to Graphic Design Methodologies and Processes

6.1
Bauhaus
Curriculum Diagram
1923
Johannes Itten

6.2
Cover for
The Dada Painters
1951
Paul Rand

6.3
Diagram from
The Measure of Man
1955
Henry Dreyfuss

Integration

Intuition

Systems

	1900			1945		
Movements and Schools	Constructivism 1915–1940		Bauhaus 1919–1933	International Typographic Style 1945–1970		Identity Des 1950s–
		Dada 1916–1920	De Stijl 1917–1931			
Theories and Thought	Structuralism 1916– Saussure		Semiotics 1938– Morris			
		Utility	Utopianism	**Systems**	Universality	Intuition
Writings and Gatherings				*The Language of Vision* (1944) Gyorgy Kepes	Apsen Conference established 1949	
				Thoughts on Design (1947) Paul Rand		
Individuals and Collaborations	Lazlo Moholy-Nagy			Otto Neurath		Paul Rand
	AIGA founded 1914				Henry Dreyfuss	Ray and Charles Eames
Events and Changes	Ford Mass Production 1910		World's Fair 1937	WW II 1939–1945	American suburbanization 1948–	
		First transistor patent issued 1928	Photocopier invented 1937			Microchip invented 1959

6.4
Department of Transportation
symbols
1974
Roger Cook and Don Shanosky

6.5
Graphical interface
Macintosh computer
1984
Steve Jobs, Jef Raskin, and Susan Kare

6.6
IDEO
*Method Card*s
2003
IDEO

ɔtics   New Media   User-Centered

| 1968 | 1984 | 2000 | + |

Deconstructive Typography
1980s–

Information Design
1960s–

Interaction Design
1990s–

-structuralism 1965– ault	Deconstruction 1967– Derrida	**Observation**	Relational Aesthetics 1998– Bourriaud
Problem Solving	Strategy Collaboration	Play DIY	**User-Centered Design**
School of Design			Web blogs 1997–
Design Methods Conference 1962	*Emigre* (1984–2005)		*Looking Closer* Series (1995–)
Icograda founded 1963	GDEA 1990–1996	IDEO	Donald Norman/Jakob Nielsen
Otl Aicher Jay Doblin		Design for Democracy	PhD in Design

U.S. civil rights legislation
passed 1964

Globalization accelerates   Cold War ends
1990s–   1991

9/11 terrorism
2001

Apple Macintosh   Adobe software
introduced 1984   introduced 1987

Public Internet
emerges 1993

John Bowers Introduction to Graphic Design Methodologies and Processes

Terms

19 **Audience**
Audience refers to the receiver of a message. An audience can be targeted or open-ended, narrow or broad, familiar or unfamiliar (with content or content navigational devices such as a website interface), and treated as passive observers or active participants.

54 **Brainstorming**
Formalized by Alex F. Osborn in the early 1950s, brainstorming is the fast, criticism-free generation of ideas.

16 **Codes**
Codes are symbols that lead to interpretations, such as those for gender roles. They may be created through the use of color to reinforce stereotypes (e.g., pink for girls, blue for boys), or suggest new viewpoints.

34 **Collaboration**
Collaboration is the process of sharing and working with others toward a common goal.

50 **Common Sense**
Common-sense decisions and opinions are based on experience, intuition, and prior learning.

51 **Concept**
A concept is a thought, notion, or idea upon which a project is based and through which a problem is solved.

48 **Constraints**
Constraints are the parameters that bound a project. These can include deadlines imposed by the designer or client, laws and ordinances, and cultural conventions or norms.

23 **Critical Thinking**
The term critical thinking comes from the Greek word *kriterion*, which means a position from which to make a judgment. Critical thinking describes thinking that is active and engaged. It examines credibility, biases, accuracy, strengths, relevance of information, questions, and assumptions.

24 **Cues**
Cues are visual identifiers that signal an action or help form an interpretation. Underlined text on a website, for example, is a cue indicating that the text is a clickable link.

Terms

55 **Decision Tree**
A decision tree is a visual pathway that provides "either-or" and "if-then" options.

16 **Decoding**
Decoding is the process of analyzing a message and determining its meaning. Decoding is influenced by the physical location and cultural context of a message, as well as the receiver's decoding abilities and familiarity with the message and its visual language.

25 **Denotation and Connotation**
Denotation refers to the physical appearance of an object: A square is a shape with four equal sides. Connotation refers to an interpretation of an object: A square can suggest neutrality or stability.

58 **Directions**
In the context of graphic design, directions can indicate multiple ways of visually solving a problem.

35 **Do It Yourself (DIY)**
DIY is a movement in which individuals with little or no training create, improve, and invent without the direct help of professionals.

16 **Encoding**
Encoding is the process of creating forms with signals and cues that can guide a response.

03 **Epistemology**
This branch of philosophy studies knowledge, questioning what it is and how it is acquired.

36 **Ethnography**
Ethnography is a method of research that observes, documents, and analyzes people interacting with designed objects and experiences in normal everyday situations. This research can provide designers with the information to improve their investigations.

43 **Evaluation**
Evaluation is the systematic assessment of a work's value.

Terms

37 **Flowcharts**
A flowchart is a diagram that shows the decision-making process of a person involved in a particular activity, such as shopping or interacting with digital media.

38 **Focus Groups**
Focus groups are collections of individuals assembled by a strategist.

51 **Function**
Function is a form's practical, spiritual, cultural, or personal purpose. An evaluation of function includes asking why the form was created, who its audience is, how it will be used, and what it will do.

58 **Generative Work**
Generative work builds upon itself, creating new ideas and outcomes in the process.

36 **Human-Centered Design**
Human-centered design is based on an understanding of user patterns and abilities. It focuses on designing objects and interactions that are rooted in observed experiences.

58 **Iteration**
An iteration is the repetition of a sequence of operations.

22 **Knowledge Domain**
A knowledge domain refers to a field of knowledge.

04 **Learning by Doing**
This theory refers to gaining knowledge through practice, by repeating a set or sets of actions to improve the outcome over time.

10 **Logic**
Logic is the study of reasoning.

25 **Metaphors**
Metaphors use words or images to suggest a likeness to another object or concept.

Terms

Terms

20 **Representation**
Representation is created through aspects of signs. In this context, a sign is a visual concept, not necessarily a physical sign.

03 **Research**
In the broadest sense, research is the search for knowledge and advancement in a deliberate and engaged, if not systematic, manner.

25 **Signs**
A sign is an image, symbol, sound, or word (signifer) that indicates a meaning (signified).

61 **Storytelling**
Storytelling is the act of relating and sharing ideas from a given point of view. Stories traditionally have a beginning, middle, and end through which elements or characters are introduced and interact as the plot unfolds. Storytelling is a timeless activity evolved from early cultural rituals used to inform, persuade, explain, and entertain.

18 **Theory**
Theory refers to groupings of ideas that seek to explain a phenomenon, guide investigation, or form an interpretation.

39 **Visual Audit**
A visual audit involves the collection and analysis of visual materials representing a company or organization.

24 **Visual Language**
Visual language refers to a message's visual elements, their arrangement and emphasis, and what they reference. It is a combination of style, taste, aesthetics, and strategy.

24 **Visual Literacy**
Visual literacy is the ability to interpret, evaluate, and derive meaning from images.

55 **Visual Matrix**
A visual matrix is a series of quadrants in which images (literal, abstract, or symbolic) and words are placed that describe aspects of a theme, subject, or object.

John Bowers Introduction to Graphic Design Methodologies and Processes

Study Questions Chapter Concepts

The following study questions will help you better comprehend the book's concepts and further your ability to apply them. None of the questions asks you to recite what you've read. Instead, they prompt you to reflect on concepts and then demonstrate your understanding through action.

You will be asked to go to a public space, observe, document, or interview, or research a methodology or process from sources listed in the bibliography, and respond by analyzing and making. During the process, the opportunity exists to clarify ideas, gain additional knowledge, and merge concepts from across chapters.

The questions allow you to draw from your own experiences and immediate environment as a way of building upon existing knowledge, and to demonstrate the prevalence of the book's methodologies and processes across many activities. Experiencing the book's concepts firsthand is an aid to understanding them.

Study Questions Chapter Concepts

Introduction
Problem Seeking and Solving

Document the process used to prepare and serve a meal, then categorize these steps and evaluate the process.

List the steps you took to make your commute. Which steps were most critical, included feedback from others, were most influenced by outside variables, or could be eliminated?

Chapter 1
Looking Broadly

Choose a work or designer in this book that best describes your own working process, and explain how it is related.

Observe five people doing the same thing in public. Describe the object, event, and strategy they employ to achieve their desired goals. How could their processes be improved?

Chapter 2
Interpreting

List five ways the letter X, whether as a letter or a symbol, can function, then determine which expressions are culturally specific and which have alternative expressions.

Record the food products that you consume in a single day. Next, categorize and assess the value of each by comparing product costs, purposes, and functions relative to their nutritional value, carbon footprint, or recyclability.

Study Questions Chapter Concepts

Chapter 3
Targeting

Find a corporate symbol and analyze how its visual language expresses believability or reliability (quality), product or service (purpose), and status or philosophy (culture).

Document five publicly placed handmade signs (such as "lost dog" or "yard sale") and describe the visual devices (large type, compelling image, etc.) each uses to elicit the desired response.

Chapter 4
Creating

Make a visual audit of at least 10 messages found in a public location. Group and label them, then reorganize them to tell a visual story about that location.

Make a thinking map, attribute list, visualization matrix, and positioning matrix that explain how tattoos, websites, and billboards are related.

Chapter 5
Looking Closer

Describe the focus of each designer's work (e.g., description, operation, identification, or relation) and how the work of all the designers relates.

Choose one designer's work and compare it to a piece of music, architecture, film, or literature.

Timeline

Find another timeline spanning any length, superimpose it over the book's timeline, and describe how it influenced or was influenced by graphic design methodologies and processes.

John Bowers Introduction to Graphic Design Methodologies and Processes

Exercises

The following individual and collaborative exercises develop concepts presented earlier in the book. While they have set learning outcomes, they allow students to personalize the learning by asking them to draw from their own experiences.

Participants gain not only knowledge but also new social and communication skills. All of these exercises are based on ritual, but other themes or issues could be used instead, such as consumption, identity, or place. They require both left-brain (logical, sequential) and right-brain (intuitive, holistic) thinking and accommodate the variety of learning styles listed below.

· Learning Style Theory

This theory describes how "concrete perceivers" and "active processors" absorb information through direct experience, i.e., by doing, and how "abstract perceivers" and "reflective processors" understand experiences by reflecting and thinking about them.

· Vygotsky Social Cognition Theory

This theory holds that culture itself provides methods and tools for thinking. The culture and community of the classroom affect student learning.

· Communities of Practice Theory

This theory holds that learning is fundamentally social, i.e., learning environments are also social environments. The process of learning is inseparable from community membership; our identities change as learning takes place.

Exercises
Learning Outcomes
Students should be able to demonstrate the ability to:

· Critically analyze and apply conceptual development methods to accomplish specific purposes
· Analyze and articulate the role of design in chosen cultures and societies
· Collaborate with others in the generation and evaluation of concepts

6.7
Each student chooses a culturally coded object (e.g., silicon wristband or pill) and writes the object name at the top of a large sheet of paper.

Object Pill

Questions

How does it work?
Why does it cost so much?
Is the generic as effective?

Assumptions

I can trust it will work.
I will not get addicted.
I should take it.

6.8
Students write questions and assumptions about their objects.

Object Pill

Questions

- How does it work?
  Why does it cost so much?
- Is the generic as effective?
- What are the alternatives?

Assumptions

- I can trust it will work.
  I will not get addicted.
- I should take it.
- My life will be improved.

6.9
The class as a whole adds questions and assumptions, then highlights those deemed most important.

Learning Outcomes
· Gather, organize, edit, and value content
· Apply a collaborative concept generation method

Experience Assessment
· Did the process validate or put into question your listing and prioritization?
· In what areas of your object's knowledge domain are you least informed?

School of the Art Institute of Chicago 2010 Workshop Participants
· Hyojin An, Ryan Basile, Eric Baskauskas, Song Char, Akemi Hong, Hyung Kim, Melissa Parker, Ju-Ah Kwon, Hyejung Min, Youngha Park, Sungwoo Suh, Jiuxue Zhang
· John Bowers, Workshop Leader Connie White, Faculty

Listing and Prioritizing

Create and prioritize a list of questions and assumptions about a common but culturally coded object. Use the list as the basis for a visual investigation.

Process

Listing

· Write the topic at the top of a large sheet of paper.
· Write questions you have about the topic.
· List the assumptions you have about the topic.
· Have classmates add other questions and assumptions.

Prioritizing

· Indicate the most interesting questions and assumptions.
· Have classmates indicate the most interesting questions.

6.10
Students apply additional processes
to further understand their objects.

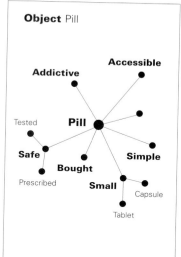

6.11
Students create thinking maps
based on their objects.

Object Pill

	Positive	Negative
	Safe	Addictive
	Effective	Difficult
	Simple	Upsetting
	Easy	Dreaded

Object Pill

		Visual	Verbal
1 Description		®	Drug
2 Identification		◯	Shape and Size
3 Operation		● ◯	Instructed Usage

6.12
Students also make an attribute
list (top) and visualization matrix
(bottom).

Learning Outcomes
· Analyze an object's utilitarian
and cultural function.
· Apply basic verbal and
visual forms of representation
and analysis.

Experience Assessment
· What information does
each of the three representation
forms convey?
· What information does this
process reveal about the chosen
object that the previous exercise
did not?

Connecting and Editing

Create a thinking map, attribute list, and visualization matrix
that identify select characteristics for visual expression.

Process

Connecting

· Choose a word and place it in the center of the page.
· Choose words by free association related to the first word.
· Choose words that describe the object.
· Choose images that describe basic aspects of the object.

Editing

· Make a list of opposite words that describe the object.

6.13
Students list the events, objects, and activities of their culture's rituals on color-coded Post-it notes.

Ritual Cultural

China

India

South Korea

Sweden

Thailand

USA

6.14
Students place the Post-it notes on a group matrix that includes the students' countries.

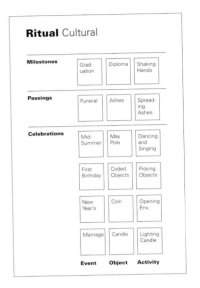

Ritual Cultural

Milestones — Graduation · Diploma · Shaking Hands

Passings — Funeral · Ashes · Spreading Ashes

Celebrations — Mid-Summer · May Pole · Dancing and Singing

First Birthday · Coded Objects · Picking Objects

New Year's · Coin · Opening Env.

Marriage · Candle · Lighting Candle

Event · Object · Activity

6.15
Collectively, the class selects, groups, and labels similar rituals, such as celebrations.

Learning Outcomes
· Apply a collaborative and flexible concept method.
· Analyze a given theme according to basic organizational categories.

Experience Assessment
· What was the influence of this physically flexible method?
· What value did collaboration bring to the process?

Umeå Institute of Design 2010 Workshop Participants
· Linda Bresäter, Ruedee Sarawutpaiboon, Tae-yeol Lim, George Paravantes, Sisirnath S, Chao Wang
· John Bowers, Workshop Leader Niklas Andersson and Linda Borgan, Faculty

Categorizing and Grouping

Analyze content by categorizing its objects, events, and activities as an aid to representing it visually.

Process

Categorizing

· Write a topic name, e.g., a ritual, at the top of a large piece of paper.
· Make a visual matrix that shows types and locations.
· Using different colored Post-it notes, write the ritual events (birthday), objects (candles), and activities (blow out candles).
· Place Post-it notes in the grid.

Grouping

· Group Post-it notes, take out duplicates, and label groups.

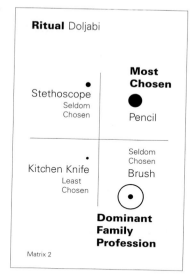

6.16
Students create a matrix based on one of their cultural rituals, e.g., the Korean Doljabi.

6.17
Selected objects of a student's Korean Doljabi birthday ritual were chosen and positioned.

6.18
The frequency with which each object was chosen and its foretelling power in a student's family history were identified.

Learning Outcomes
· Analyze, compare, and visualize a phenomenon.
· Critically value given aspects of an object, phenomenon, or interaction.

Experience Assessment
· What additional information did the positioning matrix reveal that the previous method did not?
· How could a select object such as a utensil move from one quadrant to another?

Positioning and Valuing

Make a positioning matrix that locates and values aspects of a chosen theme (e.g., a ritual) as a way of analyzing its components.

Process

Positioning

· Choose words for each intersecting line.
· Place the ritual in the appropriate quadrant.
· Place other, similar rituals in other quadrants.

Valuing

· Make the circles different sizes to show their relevance and value.

John Bowers Introduction to Graphic Design Methodologies and Processes

Endnotes

Chapter 1
Looking Broadly

1
Maruska, Mary Ann and Ulrich Wodicka, editors, "Why We Need Design Research," in *Graphic Design Journal*, Issue 4, 1996, 20.

Chapter 2
Interpreting

2
Davis, Meredith and Robin Moore, *Education through Design*. Raleigh: North Carolina Arts Council, 1993, 8.

Chapter 3
Targeting

3
Winkler, Dietmar, "Theory as an Emerging GDEA Theme Area: Guidelines, Directives and Rationales," in *GDEA Bulletin*, Fall 1992, 2.

Chapter 4
Creating

4
McMillan, Sam, "The Emotional Connection," www.apple.com/ca/pro/design/scott/index3.html

Chapter 5
Looking Closer

5 6 7
Interview with Rick Valicenti
October 2009

8 9 10
Interview with Antonio Alcalá
November 2009

11 12 13 14 15
Interview with Julie Beeler and Brad Johnson
November 2009

16 17 18 19
Interview with Michelle Bowers
November 2009

20 21 22
Interview with Sol Sender
March 2010

Bibliography

Introduction
Problem Seeking and Solving

Koberg, Don and Jim Bagnall.
The Universal Traveler. Los Altos,
CA: William Kaufmann, 1976.

De Bono, Edward.
Lateral Thinking. New York:
Harper Colophon, 1973.

Jones, John Chris.
Design Methods. Hoboken, NJ:
John Wiley & Sons, 1992.

Osburn, Alex F.
Applied Imagination. New York:
Charles Scribner's Sons, 1963.

Woolsey, Kristina Hooper,
Scott Kim, and Gayle Curtis.
VIzAbility. New York: Course
Technology, 2004.

Poggenpohl, Sharon and Keiichi
Sato, editors. *Design Integrations:
Research and Collaboration*.
New York: Intellect, Ltd., 2009.

Frascara, Jorge, Bernd Meurer,
Jan van Toorn, and Dietmar
Winkler. *User-Centred
Graphic Design*. New York:
CRC Press, 1997.

Bennett, Audrey, editor. *Design
Studies*. New York: Princeton
Architectural Press, 2006.

Chapter 1
Looking Broadly

Laurel, Brenda, editor. *Design
Research*. Cambridge, MA: MIT
Press, 2003.

Noble, Ian and Russell Bestley.
Visual Research. New York: AVA
Publishing, 2005.

O'Grady, Jennifer Visocky
and Ken O'Grady.
A Designer's Research Manual.
New York: Rockport, 2009.

Creswell, John. *Qualitative Inquiry
and Research Design:
Choosing Among Five
Approaches*. New York: Sage
Publications, 2005.

Bibliography

Chapter 2
Interpreting

Lechte, John. *Fifty Key Contemporary Thinkers: From Structuralism to Postmodernity.* London: Routledge, 1994.

Wurman, Richard Saul. *Information Anxiety.* New York: Doubleday, 1989.

Chapter 3
Targeting

IDEO. *IDEO Method Cards.* San Francisco: IDEO, 2003.

Norman, Donald. *The Psychology of Everyday Things.* New York: Basic Books, 1988.

Salen, Katie and Eric Zimmerman. *Rules of Play: Game Design Fundamentals.* Cambridge, MA: MIT Press, 2004.

The Merchants of Cool
www.pbs.org/wgbh/pages/front-line/shows/cool/

Chapter 4
Creating

Lupton, Ellen and Jennifer Cole Phillips. *Graphic Design: The New Basics.* New York: Princeton Architectural Press, 2008.

Marks, Andrea. *Writing for Visual Thinkers.* New York: AIGA, 2008.

Rand, Paul. *A Designer's Art.* New York: Yale University Press, 2000.

Tufte, Edward R. *The Visual Display of Quantitative Information.* Cheshire, CT: Graphics Press, 1992.

Venezky, Martin. *It Is Beautiful... Then Gone.* New York: Princeton Architectural Press, 2004.

Weingart, Wolfgang. *My Way to Typography.* Zurich: Lars Müller Publishers, 2000.

Chapter 5
Looking Closer

Meggs, Philip and Alston W. Purvis. *Meggs' History of Graphic Design,* 4th ed. Hoboken, NJ: John Wiley & Sons, 2005.

Eskilson, Stephen J. *Graphic Design: A New History.* New York: Yale University Press, 2007.

Design Edition
www.qfradio.org.qa/regular-programs

Design Matters
www.sterlingbrands.com/design/design_matters.php

www.aiga.org
www.designobserver.com
www.icograda.org

Design Issues
Visible Language

Index

Index

Index

John Bowers Introduction to Graphic Design Methodologies and Processes

Index

Image Credits

Cover and chapter title pages
Front and Back
Image and permission: John Bowers

Introduction
0.1
Image and permission: Visible Earth,
NASA, http:visibleearth.nasa.gov/
0.2 0.3 0.4 0.5 0.6 0.7 0.8 0.9 0.10 0.11
Image and permission: John Bowers

1
1.1
Image and permission: Gretchen Schulfer
1.2
Image and permission: John Bowers
1.3
Image and permission: IDEO
1.4 1.5
Image and permission: John Bowers
1.6
Image and permission: Second Story
Interactive Studios
1.7 1.8 1.9 1.10 1.11 1.12
Image and permission: John Bowers

2
2.1
Image and permission: Rick Valicenti
(Thirst Studio)
2.2 2.3 2.4 2.5
Image and permission: John Bowers
2.6
Top
Image and permission: John Bowers
2.6
Bottom
Image and permission: Stephen Farrell
2.7
Image and permission: John Bowers
2.8
Image and permission: AIGA
2.9
Image and permission: One Laptop Per Child
2.10
Image and permission: Stephen Farrell
2.11
Image and permission: Antonio Alcalá
2.12 2.13
Image and permission: John Bowers

2.14
Image and permission: NASA
2.15
Image and permission: Eugene Richards,
photographer
2.16
Image and permission: Concept: O. Toscani,
courtesy of United Colors of Benetton

3
3.1
Image and permission: IDEO
3.2 3.3 3.4 3.5 3.6
Image and permission: John Bowers
3.7
Image and permission: Nike, Inc.
3.8 3.9
Image and permission: John Bowers
3.10
Image: Nancy Froehlich, photographer;
permission: exhibition curated and designed
by the Graphic Design MFA Program,
Maryland Institute College of Art (MICA).
Ellen Lupton/Jennifer Cole Phillips,
directors
3.11
Image and permission: John Bowers
3.12
Image and permission: John DeVylder
3.13 3.14
Image and permission: John Bowers
3.15
Image and permission: IDEO
3.16
Image and permission: John Bowers
3.17
Image and permission: Art Institute of
Chicago
3.18 3.19 3.20 3.21 3.22
Image and permission: John Bowers
3.23
Image and permission: Second Story
Interactive Studios

Image Credits

John Bowers Introduction to Graphic Design Methodologies and Processes

Essay A Lesson from Spirograph

While recently going through some items in my mom's basement, I found the "1967 Toy of the Year." With the exception of a few missing pieces, the Spirograph I shared with my brother was almost perfectly intact: plastic circles and rings, colored pens, pins, storage tray, a piece of cardboard, a pad of white paper, and the "pattern booklet."

The still-popular, mass-produced toy from the 60s is the embodiment of controlled emotion in the face of the decade's social unrest and conflict. The Spirograph promoted adherence to procedures and noncontroversial design through a methodical process.

Originally posted on
Design Observer, May 8, 2008

Although the Spirograph provided hours of fun, wonder, and amazement for my brother and me as we formed our simple patterns, using it again as an adult has prompted a few thoughts on wonder and its limitations.

Designed by British engineer Denys Fisher in 1962 and acquired by the American manufacturer Kenner Toys in 1966, the first and simplest of many Spirograph versions hit the stores in 1967, the year we received ours as a Christmas gift. The accompanying manual stated that the toy "stimulates the imagination and develops creativity," and that there would be "no limit to the different designs you can make!"

The set has 18 sizes of small circles that fit into two large rings. Designs are created by placing a pen in a circle's holes and moving the circle inside a ring, which is pinned down in the cardboard to make it stationary. The pattern booklet shows a dozen designs and describes the required ring, circle(s), and pen positions. For example, one formula

119

(abbreviated) reads: "Pin RING no. 144/96 to Paper and Baseboard, the No. 1 mark at the top…with pen in Hole 3 draw another pattern. Repeat, using Holes 5 and 7."

The design procedure is both methodical and repeatable, with the patterns yielding virtually exact copies for all users. The most fun for us came not by following the patterns or the rules but by randomly mixing colors, moving the circles and rings at will, and placing lots of pinholes in our designs.

The Spirograph demonstrates, if not promotes, the belief that design can be formulaic and that good design has something to do with simplicity and objectivity. However, qualitative aspects such as emotion, irrationality, and instinct are largely missing. The patterns themselves make no direct reference to a user's nationality, ethnicity, social class, or gender. Choices are officially confined to color and template combinations.

The focused geometric and rational visual language and limited plastic components restrict the range of outcomes and equalize abilities. It brings to mind a Swedish saying my wife told me: "Everyone wants you to succeed, as long as you're not doing better than they are." Our designs were original but not too original.

We received our Spirograph as the space race was underway and the Cold War was yet to thaw, the summer of love was over, and the Tet Offensive was soon to begin. Soon my brother would receive his draft lottery number. Perhaps the Spirograph offered a bit of rationality and order to the chaos. It was predictable and socially safe. Any combination of templates and color would result in a Spirograph manual "sanctioned" design. The toy gave the illusion of counter-culture experimentation, yet furthered the establishment adherence to staying the course.

Yet I felt a sense of pride in the detailed patterns I could draw. It was incredible, magical, how quickly overlapping circles would create a dynamic and mesmerizing design. Even more, I was in awe of the more complex and colorful patterns my older brother could create. Perhaps he was working through the stress of receiving his impending call to duty.

What set the Spirograph apart from our other toys in that era was the suggestion that we were actually creating art. Drawing patterns was more than simply assembling parts in various combinations to create a temporary object to be taken apart (e.g., Legos) or moving a stylus to create a temporary design to be erased (e.g., Etch-A-Sketch).

Allowing repeatable solutions, minimizing differences, and channeling outcomes in part describe the 1967 Toy of the Year. Denys Fisher's design was an outgrowth of his work on Vietnam-era munitions, research no doubt guided by procedures and constraints.

Thankfully, my brother made it through the Vietnam War without getting drafted, and we recently played a round of Spirograph together. At the bottom of the box were some patterns we had drawn 41 years earlier. Looking back, I clearly saw how limits can provide a sanctuary, foster exploration, and, with some imagination, generate beauty. But the random pinholes in the official paper pad reinforce the notion that sometimes moving outside of what's expected has its place, too.

John Bowers Introduction to Graphic Design Methodologies and Processes

Notes

John Bowers Introduction to Graphic Design Methodologies and Processes

MARK GALLAGHER

THE BUSINESS OF WINNING

STRATEGIC SUCCESS FROM THE
FORMULA ONE TRACK TO THE BOARDROOM

KoganPage

LONDON PHILADELPHIA NEW DELHI

First published in Great Britain and the United States in 2014 by Kogan Page Limited

2nd Floor, 45 Gee Street	1518 Walnut Street, Suite 1100	4737/23 Ansari Road
London EC1V 3RS	Philadelphia PA 19102	Daryaganj
United Kingdom	USA	New Delhi 110002
www.koganpage.com		India

© Mark Gallagher, 2014

The right of Mark Gallagher to be identified as the author of this work has been asserted by him in accordance with the Copyright, Designs and Patents Act 1988.

ISBN   978 0 7494 7272 6
E-ISBN   978 0 7494 7273 3

British Library Cataloguing-in-Publication Data

A CIP record for this book is available from the British Library.

Library of Congress Cataloging-in-Publication Data

Gallagher, Mark, 1962-
   The business of winning : strategic success from the Formula One track to the boardroom / Mark Gallagher.
      pages cm
      ISBN 978-0-7494-7272-6 (paperback) – ISBN 978-0-7494-7273-3 (ebk)
1. Grand prix racing–Management.   2. Management.   3. Leadership.   I. Title.
   GV1029.14.G35 2014
   796.72–dc23
                                                                                    2014026698

Typeset by Graphicraft Limited, Hong Kong
Print production managed by Jellyfish
Printed and bound by CPI Group (UK) Ltd, Croydon, CR0 4YY